100 SHOES

Front cover: *"Portrait" Shoes.* Vivienne Westwood, British, b. 1941. Leather, 1990.
Millia Davenport and Zipporah Fleisher Fund, 2006   2006.14a, b

Back cover: *Evening boot designed by Roger Vivier.* Photograph: Paul Schutzer/Time & Life Pictures/Getty Images

Published by The Metropolitan Museum of Art in association with Yale University Press

Produced by the Department of Special Publications, The Metropolitan Museum of Art: Robie Rogge, Publishing Manager; Linda Falken, Senior Editor; Atif Toor, Designer; Victoria Gallina, Production.

Text for shoes in the Brooklyn Museum Costume Collection at The Metropolitan Museum of Art by Glenn Petersen.

Photography for shoes in the Brooklyn Museum Costume Collection at The Metropolitan Museum of Art by Lea Ingold.
All other photography by The Metropolitan Museum of Art Photograph Studio, unless otherwise noted in the credits.

First Edition

Printed in China

20 19 18 17 16 15 14 13 12 11   5 4 3 2 1

Library of Congress Control Number: 2011926881

ISBN 978-1-58839-416-3 (The Metropolitan Museum of Art)
ISBN 978-0-300-17240-9 (Yale University Press)

The Metropolitan Museum of Art
1000 Fifth Avenue
New York, NY 10028-0198
212.570.3894
www.metmuseum.org

Yale University Press
302 Temple Street
P.O. Box 209040
New Haven, CT 06520-9040
www.yalebooks.com

100 SHOES

THE COSTUME INSTITUTE
THE METROPOLITAN MUSEUM OF ART

THE METROPOLITAN MUSEUM OF ART, NEW YORK
YALE UNIVERSITY PRESS, NEW HAVEN AND LONDON

INTRODUCTION

When I was asked to write the introduction to *100 Shoes*, my reaction was "Only 100?" Considering that so much history and style are represented in the 2,500 shoes at The Metropolitan Museum of Art's Costume Institute, I didn't know how the curators could possibly choose only 100 pairs from such a vast collection of the most exotic, enduring, and elegant footwear.

The broad range of designers makes identifying the iconic masterworks a real challenge. As I flip through the images, I see some of my favorites—Manolo Blahnik, Alexander McQueen, Christian Louboutin—but also many discoveries from long ago and far away. Rather than browsing shoes in a store, seeing them in a book or museum lets us appreciate them as works of art with a place in culture and history, and also as mechanisms to elevate the style, stature, and status of women around the world.

Sarah Jessica Parker at The Costume Institute Gala Benefit celebrating the opening of "American Woman: Fashioning a National Identity" at The Metropolitan Museum of Art.

French shoe,
1690–1700

At Met exhibitions, we glimpse shoes on the "American Woman," "The Model as Muse," and "Superheroes," or see paintings of eighteenth-century aristrocrats wearing the shoes of their era. If truly lucky, a curator friend might show us vintage Viviers in specially designed drawers. In May, walking up the Met's steps into The Costume Institute Gala Benefit, I love to see what everyone is wearing from head to toe, especially after selecting the ideal shoes for my McQueen or Halston gown. But being able to sit on the sofa at home and look back through time at 100 expertly chosen shoes makes for a whole different kind of treat.

As an essential fashion accessory, shoes allow us to manipulate our attitude and height, change our look, express our passion. *100 Shoes* shows a range of objects from the sixteenth to the twenty-first century, including some that remind me of my favorite shapes and silhouettes, many with unexpected and more obscure histories. Platform shoes, for example, are nothing new. Venetian women wore them from the fifteenth to the seventeenth century, and Manchu Chinese women wore them in the 1800s. In the late 1930s, Salvatore Ferragamo introduced

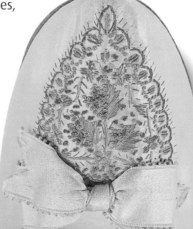

Court presentation
shoe, 1896

modern platforms, and these height-enhancers have remained popular, with notable resurgences in the 1970s and again in the 1990s, courtesy of Vivienne Westwood.

Sandals go back at least 5,500 years to the ancient Egyptians, who made them out of papyrus, palm leaves, grass, reeds, and even solid gold. In the West, sandals declined in the seventeenth century and didn't reemerge until the late 1930s.

Stilettos have a history that began well before Manolo's time. Popular with aristocratic European women in the sixteenth and seventeenth centuries, high heels fell out of favor after the French Revolution. Low heels and flats were the It-Shoe until the mid-1800s, when heels rose again. They've remained in style, in varying heights and shapes, ever since.

Platforms, sandals, and stilettos, plus an array of other showstoppers, are highlights of a shoe collection that inspires us to assert our style and power.

—Sarah Jessica Parker

Christian Louboutin platform shoe, 2008

Chopines
1550–1650
Probably Italian

T he raised thick-soled shoes known as chopines first appeared in fifteenth-century Venice as an upper-class fashion that had both a practical and a symbolic function. Taller versions covered with suede or leather are thought to have been worn outdoors for protection from irregularly paved and muddy streets, while those of more perishable materials were worn indoors. Both versions indicated the elevated social status of their wearers.

The chopines shown here are covered in a rich velvet decorated with gold braid edging and a beardlike tassel below the open toe. The lobed platform sole is trimmed in gold lace with hobnails, and the vamp, with shirred ribbon.

The height of chopines made it difficult for women to walk, so they were usually accompanied by attendants on whom they could balance. Gradually, very high chopines became associated with the courtesan, whose thus-increased stature served to draw attention to herself.

Marie-Anne-Christine-Victoire of Bavaria, wife of Louis XIV's eldest child, is shown with two of their sons in this detail of a painting by Pierre Mignard (French, 1612–1695). The pointed toe of one elegant shoe is visible beneath her skirt.

Shoes
1690–1700
French

During the long reign (1643–1715) of Louis XIV, the French court championed elaborately ornamented clothing and accessories. In the same way that *robes à la française* were designed to showcase luxurious embroideries and silk damask fabric, women's shoes provided a canvas for the period's woven artistry.

The embroidered floral design on this pair of shoes is pleasingly rendered, and the stitching along the sole and heel adds an appealing element of contrast. The high tongue, pointed toe, and domed sole are typical of fashionable ladies' shoes of the era, and the red heels indicate that the former owner was a noblewoman. Louis XIV, who always wore red high heels, decreed that only members of his royal court could do the same.

Latchet Shoes
1750–69

British

T he bold, colorful, and finely worked flame-stitch uppers are an immediate eye-catcher on these latchet shoes. A common embroidery style, flame-stitch canvas work is preserved in upholstery and small accessories from the period, although the shoe at left has an unusual level of variety in the pattern. Its printed silk heel is also atypical, as printed silks were uncommon and seldom used for footwear.

The evolution of the fashionable silhouette can be seen when this shoe, dated to 1750–69, is compared with the pair of flame-stitch shoes from 1720–29 at right. In the former example, the heel is higher and more upright, the toe is blunter and less upturned, the sole is flatter, the throat is lower, and the metallic braid trim seen in the center of the vamp on the older pair has disappeared.

Slippers
1790–1805

Probably British

Large shoe buckles had begun to go out of style in the 1780s, but their demise was radically accelerated by the anti-aristocratic sentiments of the French Revolution (1789–99). The way was then clear for the slipper to supplant the latchet shoe as the primary style of fashionable women's wear. Strong or dark colorations were often worn with the white dresses seen around the turn of the nineteenth century, and the attractive teal blue color of the slipper shown here was one of the favorite choices.

In *Young Woman Drawing,* an 1801 painting by Marie-Denise Villers (French, 1774–1821), the subject is dressed in the style popular at the time: a simple white dress with an empire waist, a mull fichu, or kerchief, and strongly colored slippers.

Lotus Shoes
1800–1943
Chinese

F oot-binding, a custom begun in the tenth century and lasting into the twentieth, was widely practiced among Chinese women. The ideal length of the golden lotus, as the bound foot was euphemistically called, was three inches or less.

Young girls from the ages of four to seven began the two-year binding process while their bones were still malleable. The four smaller toes were bent under the foot, and the forepart of the foot was folded back until it nearly touched the heel.

The style of lotus shoes varied from region to region, particularly in the shaping of the sole. The bootlike shoes shown at left are of satin trimmed with embroidery and bands of fancy-weave ribbon.

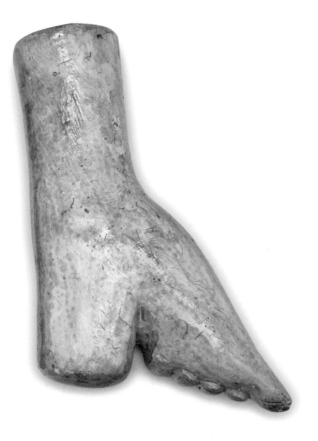

This plaster model of a bound foot illustrates how the toes were turned under and the foot folded back toward the heel.

Pedestal Shoes
19th century
Chinese (Manchu peoples)

The Manchu peoples did not subscribe to the custom of foot-binding practiced widely throughout China. Manchu footwear, for both men and women, had its own special characteristics, however. Although the foot itself was not reshaped, the soles were elevated on platforms two to four inches high. Women's shoes, like the one shown at left were more elaborately decorated than men's, with bright embroidery on colored silk. The hooflike shape of the pedestal served to stabilize the wearer.

In this 1903 photograph, the Empress Dowager Cixi's feet can be seen below her hem. When she was standing, only the whitened soles of her pedestal shoes would be visible, giving the impression of diminished support for her body. In their own way, Manchu platforms conformed to and conveyed the Chinese preference for a tiny foot and a tentative gait.

Slippers
ca. 1825

British

As the countries of Europe spread their empires across the globe, accounts of the exotic peoples of foreign lands captivated the audiences at home. Along with other indigenous peoples, Native Americans were romanticized by white society, particularly in Europe. Demonstrating that interest, these British slippers are an unusually close imitation of Native American moccasins such as those at right. Despite this resemblance, however, the slippers are made entirely with European construction techniques: Native buckskin has been replaced by satin and flannel, quillwork ornamentation has been reproduced in thread embroidery, and authentic moccasin construction has been replaced by turn-shoe construction with a hard sole.

Ankle Boots and Pattens
1825–30

American

B y the 1820s, ankle boots were becoming the favored daytime footwear for ladies
in both the United States and Europe, especially for taking long walks, a practice
known as pedestrianism. Like the shoes of the time, however, fashionable boots were
often constructed of flimsy materials, which made for difficult walking on cobbled
or unpaved roads. As a minor concession to utility, pattens were worn over
the thin-soled boots, providing a heavier sole for walking. Since pattens
were basically utilitarian, it is somewhat unusual for them to survive
in good condition, and even rarer to find a pair matching the
boots with which they were worn.

Early pointe shoes were modified satin evening slippers with ribbon ties. In the mid-1800s, Maria Taglioni became one of the first ballerinas to consistently dance *en pointe* without the aid of wires to hold her up. Unlike today's pointe shoes, Taglioni's did not have a hard block in the toes, so she had to rely on the strength in her own feet and ankles.

Evening Slippers
1835–45

Probably American

During the first three decades of the nineteenth century, flat evening slippers were worn in both bright and pastel colors. As tastes changed and skirts lengthened to obscure the feet, black and white satin slippers became predominant. The grass green of this pair of shoes was one of the few bright colors that continued to be seen into the 1840s. This basic form remained the standard evening slipper for decades, and one can see the distinctive wide, square toe that prevailed from the 1820s to the 1870s.

In this detail from an 1864 fashion plate, a short lace-up boot can be seen peeping from under the wide skirt of the young woman on the right.

Evening Boots
1860–69

French

When the cage crinoline replaced starched and corded petticoats in the mid-1800s, skirts swayed back and forth as women moved, revealing more ankle than was considered proper. Short boots solved the problem. They were worn regularly by day and were an option for evening. This pair of evening boots is typical except for especially refined curved lines at the ankle and top edge. The large rosette on each boot adds ornament and interest to the otherwise plain surface. Front lacing was predominant until the 1870s, when it was superseded by button closures.

Slippers
ca. 1870

Julien Mayer, French

Despite their rather grand appearance, these fancy slippers would have been suitable only for daytime wear around the house and when receiving intimate friends. In Victorian times, when a lady ventured out of the house, she wore boots, and in the evening or when receiving guests more formally, heeled shoes. Bows at the throat of the shoe became fashionable in the 1860s and grew in size to cover the instep by the end of the decade. This pair of slippers stands out for its high quality, attractive choice of contrasting materials, and good state of preservation.

Opposite page:
The bows that were so popular at the time can be seen on the subject's slippers in this 1862 painting by Édouard Manet (French, 1832–1883).

Carriage Boots
1870–90

American

Carriage boots protected the feet during chilly carriage rides. Worn over delicate evening shoes, they were often lined or trimmed with fur and featured a slit front that allowed them to be easily put on and taken off.

This pair of boots is unusually ornate and visually appealing by virtue of the colorful and boldly patterned uppers. The velvet fabric is, in fact, a wide ribbon, probably upholstery trim, which has been pieced together horizontally. By the mid-1800s, left and right shoes were becoming more common; however, straight lasts were used to make these boots, allowing each one to be worn on either foot. The original laces on the boots have been replaced.

Carriage boots or foot warmers as well as hats, coats, scarves, muffs, and lap robes were essential for winter travel in an unheated carriage or a sleigh, as shown in this detail of an 1877–94 Currier & Ives print—and for those who could afford it, fur was the material of choice.

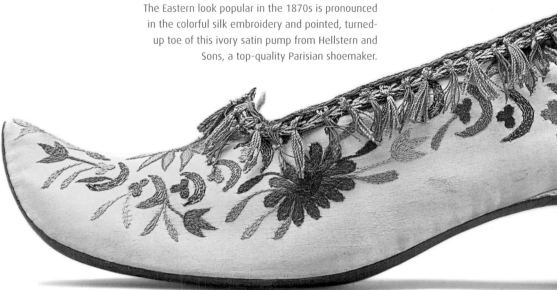

The Eastern look popular in the 1870s is pronounced in the colorful silk embroidery and pointed, turned-up toe of this ivory satin pump from Hellstern and Sons, a top-quality Parisian shoemaker.

Pumps
1873

French

I n the first half of the nineteenth century, women's shoes and boots with flat soles were fashionable, but by the 1870s, mules and slippers with heels had returned. Embroidery, beading, ribbonwork, and canvas work frequently appear on surviving shoes from this period. At left, the exquisite satin square-toed pump made by J. A. Petit, Paris, features Eastern motifs embroidered in silk and gold metallic threads. The rich colors attest to the widespread use of aniline dyes by the second half of the nineteenth century.

Evening Shoes
1875–85

French

As was not uncommon at the time for wealthy American women, Abigail Kinsley Norman Prince, wife of Frederick H. Prince, Jr., a prominent financier, traveled to Paris to acquire the most fashionable and expertly crafted clothing available. Among her acquisitions were these two pairs of evening shoes exemplifying French high style with their atypical cut and refined decoration. The shoes on the left are decorated with glass-bead embroidery in a foliate design, while the exquisite ribbonwork and chenille embroidery in the pair at right produces an interesting three-dimensional effect.

Ankle-tie shoes were fashionable in the late 1870s and 1880s but do not appear to have been widely worn. This hybrid style can be seen as a compromise between evening slippers and the satin boots that were then popular for evening wear.

Evening Slippers
1880

J. Ferry, French

Interpretations of historical styles were popular with fashionable women of the nineteenth century because of their artistic and aristocratic associations. Revivals of Baroque and Rococo styles started to appear in shoes in the 1860s. With uppers fashioned from silk fabric replicating Rococo brocade, Louis heels, and latchetlike bows, these slippers are updated versions of the fashionable eighteenth-century style in footwear.

J. Ferry was one of the most exclusive Parisian shoemakers of the late nineteenth century. Handmade to match a dress of the same fabric, the slippers were meticulously crafted so that the placement of the lace and floral pattern motifs is identical on each one.

Evening Boots
1885–90

Probably French

W hile the slipper and the strapped shoe were the most common choices for evening wear in the last third of the nineteenth century, boots did occasionally still appear. As with shoes, the basic evening boot was satin, either plain or featuring an embroidered vamp, usually in floral or foliate designs. Surviving examples of evening boots from the late nineteenth and early twentieth centuries suggest, however, that women who were daring enough to wear something already outside the ordinary often opted for unconventionally bold and unusual materials and trimmings. This pair of boots typifies that phenomenon: anachronistic side-lacing and metal ic embroidery covering the entire boot, including the heel, in atypically exuberant fret and scroll motifs.

Evening Shoes
1889–93

American

S old by A. J. Cammeyer, one of the largest shoe retailers in New York, this remarkable pair of oxfords can be firmly dated to 1889–93, as indicated by the style and by the store address on the label. The use of gold kid was extremely unusual at this date, as it was not until the 1920s that metallic leathers became common for women's evening shoes. It is even more unexpected to find a laced shoe—traditionally a day-wear style—in this material, and while low tie-shoes did come into vogue for dressy wear about 1905, even that cut did not approach the full oxford seen here. Extraordinary footwear such as this challenges the conventional view of fashion history, and it is hard to imagine for what occasion the shoes would have been worn.

Juliet Slippers
ca. 1892
American

The Juliet shoe (and its masculine incarnation, the Romeo shoe) with its high front and back and low V at the sides was introduced in the early 1890s. By the turn of the twentieth century, it had become one of the standard slipper cuts. This early example in red grained leather features tassels at the ends of the long curving points, which have been exaggerated to a comical extent. The slippers' whimsical design and loose fit indicate that they were intended to be worn at home.

Court Presentation Shoes
1896

American or European

These shoes, with their Louis heels and delicate embroidery on the straps and toes, were made to match the opulent formal gown worn by Emily Warren Roebling in 1896 for her presentation to Queen Victoria as well as for the coronation of Nicholas II and Alexandra Fyodorovna of Russia that same year. Emily Warren was married to Washington Augustus Roebling, who became chief engineer of the Brooklyn Bridge after his father's death. After her husband developed a disease now known as decompression sickness, Emily Roebling took over the on-site supervision of the project until the bridge's completion in 1883.

Emily Roebling wore her court presentation dress when she had her portrait painted by Charles-Émile-Auguste Carolus-Duran (French, 1838–1917) in 1896.

Pumps
ca. 1906

J. Ferry, French

Colorful footwear was in vogue in the relatively flamboyant 1890s, but by the turn of the century, black, brown, and white had become the appropriate hues for day wear. Other colors were reserved for evening or special occasions. The dressy red low-cut pumps at left, with mock ties at the throat, were meticulously handmade by J. Ferry, one of the most exclusive shoemakers working in Paris at the time, for a wealthy American client, Abigail Kinsley Norman Prince.

A pair of similarly styled pumps, made in America in 1900 and also owned by Mrs. Prince, was executed in metallic gold kid, a practice uncommon before 1900 and not widespread until the 1920s.

Pumps
1913–18

Pietro Yantorny, Italian, 1874–1936

T he placard outside Pietro Yantorny's shoe salon in Paris read *Le bottier le plus cher du monde,* or "The most expensive shoemaker in the world." Though Yantorny's shoes were expensive, they were also exquisitely crafted, and it could take him as long as two years to complete a single pair.

This silk pump has a woven floral pattern in the early eighteenth-century Baroque style. The Louis heel, pointed toe, long vamp, and standing tongue decorated with a large rhinestone buckle at the instep are characteristic Yantorny details.

Pietro Yantorny

Italian, 1874–1936

Pietro Yantorny was a consummate craftsman devoted to the art of shoemaking. He sought to create the most finely crafted shoes possible for a select clientele of perfectly dressed people. Because Yantorny did not advertise and his production was strictly limited, his work is now best known to Americans through surviving shoes he created for Rita de Acosta Lydig, who reportedly owned more than three hundred pairs. Alluring and individualistic, Lydig was an ideal client for Yantorny: dedicated to the art of self-presentation, profligate in her clothing expenditures, and very, very rich.

An avid collector of antique lace and textiles, Rita de Acosta Lydig probably supplied the lace on this pair of evening shoes from 1914–19. Yantorny applied identical motifs to several pairs of shoes in precisely the same pattern, which would have required cutting out the pieces from a significantly larger section of lace.

This collection of Yantorny shoes, along with their custom-made shoe trees and trunk, now at The Costume Institute, originally belonged to Lydig.

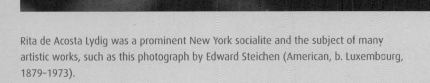

Rita de Acosta Lydig was a prominent New York socialite and the subject of many artistic works, such as this photograph by Edward Steichen (American, b. Luxembourg, 1879–1973).

Mules
1914–19
Pietro Yantorny, Italian, 1874–1936

The style of these mules, an interpretation of the *babouche,* the traditional heelless Turkish slipper associated with the harem, was especially appropriate for the boudoir. Similar to that on Turkish examples, the fabric has been embroidered *à la disposition* to conform to the final three-dimensional design. Pietro Yantorny created the slippers for one of his best clients, Rita de Acosta Lydig, whose idiosyncratic taste in fashion embraced an Orientalist aesthetic.

The first great work painted by Eugène Delacroix (French, 1798–1863) after a trip to Morocco was *Women of Algiers in Their Apartment* (1834). Traditional Turkish slippers can be seen in the foreground of this detail from the painting.

Evening Boots
ca. 1918
American

In the nineteenth century, high shoes with a strapped or laced front were called Grecian boots or Grecian sandals. In about 1913, however, a new name appeared: the tango boot. The dance craze of the 1910s encouraged footwear that was both showy and firmly secured to the foot, thus elevating the tango boot and its sister style, the tango shoe (a pump with crossing laces or straps that extended up the ankle), to prominence. The flamboyant metallic material of this tango boot from the Bray Bros. department store in Philadelphia was certain to attract attention to the movement of the feet, whether on or off the dance floor.

Tango boots were worn by the woman dancer in this advertising poster, which was created by Georges Redon (French, 1869–1943) in about 1914.

Evening Shoes
ca. 1920
American

During the heyday of American shoe manufacturing (roughly 1870 to 1930), Brooklyn was such an important center of stylish shoe production that high-fashion shoes were known in the industry as "Brooklyn Shoes." Preserved as a manufacturer's sample by the borough's Charles Strohbeck company, the unworn pair of modish, mid-range T-strap shoes at right clearly illustrates the style of fashionable shoes made from 1918 to 1922: an extremely pointed toe, narrow elongated lines, and high, narrow arch breaking in a sharp angle at the ball of the foot.

With the emergence of short skirts in the later 1910s and the 1920s, shoe design suddenly became more important to fashion, and designers offered a variety of new ideas and materials. Both the figured fabric imitating embroidery on the T-straps and the blue-gray crackle-patterned leather on the shoes at left, also from Strohbeck, were unusual choices.

"Le Bal" Slippers
1924

André Perugia, French, 1893–1977,
for Paul Poiret, French, 1879–1944

This magnificent pair of evening slippers, created for couturier Paul Poiret's wife, Denise, is completely embroidered in colored seed beads. The Poirets are portrayed, one on the vamp of each shoe, creating a sensation as they enter a crowded ball. Made by the great cobbler André Perugia, the slippers are in the style of a simple pump except for the exaggerated tongue that evokes the early eighteenth-century court of Louis XIV. Poiret's preference for high color and dramatic shapes was appropriate for the world of high society, epitomized by the images of him and his wife gliding through its glittering precincts.

Shoes
1925–30
Pietro Yantorny, Italian, 1874–1936

Lace-up shoes with strappy cutouts are a classic 1920s day style, and this example is finely detailed with wave-cut seams and hand-stitched bar tacks for the closure. Pietro Yantorny invented the looped lacing system seen on these shoes in 1916 and was granted a United States patent in 1920. His system was intended to improve fit and comfort, eliminate bulk, reduce wear on the laces and make it easier to replace them, and, in closed shoes, to provide superior rain protection. The elegant and distinctive curve of the inside heel is a hallmark of Yantorny shoes.

Evening Shoes
ca. 1927
American

As hemlines rose to the knees in the 1920s, shoe design gained in importance. To accompany the glittering flapper dresses of the time, shoe designers often used metallic leathers and lively appliqués. This flamboyant pair of T-strap shoes made in Paris for the Marshall Field department store is extraordinary for its flashy offbeat colors and pearlized leather as well as for its meticulously applied gold kid piping. At the intersection of the T on the instep, sparkling pavé rhinestones would have called additional attention to the wearer's beautifully shod feet.

In this 1920s photograph, Juliette Compton, an actress and performer in the Ziegfeld Follies, is shown wearing a flapper-style dress and shoes.

Oxfords
ca. 1927
British

First appearing in men's shoes about 1800, oxfords have been a staple of the female wardrobe for more than a hundred years. While many women's oxfords are almost indistinguishable from men's, they have often been feminized with a high heel. In the early 1900s, wealthy American women who could travel to Europe to stock up on the tailored suits then in vogue often chose Britain as the source for complementary footwear, as did the woman who purchased the high-quality, custom-made oxfords from Thomas of London shown here. Her order for eight pairs of the shoes in different colors and materials attests to the classic quality of the style.

Evening Sandals
1928–29

André Perugia, French, 1893–1977

André Perugia's elegant and innovative footwear has earned him a place among the finest shoe designers of the twentieth century. For more than sixty years, Perugia collaborated with top couturiers, most notably Paul Poiret in the 1910s and 1920s and Elsa Schiaparelli in the 1930s. This pair of evening sandals, with its cast-metal heel and exquisite metal buckle in a wreath motif, represents the height of progressive design and craftsmanship for which Perugia was known. The daringly bare open back was extremely advanced, if not shocking, for the period.

André Perugia's extraordinary gilt-metal heel was cast in the ornate mode of Art Deco artisans.

Evening Shoes
1935–40
American

Targeting wealthy socialites and celebrities as his customers, Herman Delman opened a custom shoe shop on Madison Avenue in 1919. Gradually shifting to manufacturing, Delman hired top designers, most notably Roger Vivier, to create finely crafted, chic, and luxurious footwear. A savvy promoter, Delman pioneered the practice of featuring film stars in his ads and partnered with exclusive clothing stores, including Saks and Bergdorf Goodman, to distribute his shoes. Contrary to common practice, Delman insisted that his name appear in every shoe he manufactured, thus securing his company's reputation and success. This tour-de-force pair of slightly oversize shoes was probably made for exhibition purposes. The extraordinary incised and painted plastic heels feature the coat of arms of the City of Paris with the motto *Fluctuat nec mergitur*: "It is tossed by the waves but does not sink."

Pumps
1935–49

French

Boudoir slippers were standard items of apparel for the fashionable woman from the eighteenth to the early twentieth century. By the 1930s, they were an anachronism, but fantasy shoes, as represented by this pair of pumps made with silver metallic leather, would have been appropriate for at-home entertaining. The embossed and hand-painted mosaic pattern and peaks at toe, throat, and heel give the shoes a flavor of what was then considered Eastern exoticism.

Platform Sandals
1938

Salvatore Ferragamo, Italian, 1898–1960

Taking inspiration from the chopines that were popular from the fifteenth to the seventeenth century, master Italian shoemaker Salvatore Ferragamo pioneered the development of the wedge heel and platform sole. Both were made possible by his invention of a specially designed cork wedge, which he patented in 1937. The rainbow-hued ankle-strap sandal shown at right is a style that was originally created for Judy Garland. In the 1940s, platform shoes would be designed with a high arch, but here, despite the height added by the platform, the heel is only a little higher than the toes. One of the most elaborate examples of Ferragamo's platform sandals, the evening style at left was available at Saks Fifth Avenue for one hundred dollars, an exorbitant price for a pair of sandals at the time.

Salvatore Ferragamo

Italian, 1898–1960

Salvatore Ferragamo made his first pair of shoes at the age of nine with borrowed tools from a local shoemaker. He spent a year studying in Naples, and by the time Ferragamo was fourteen, he was running his own workshop specializing in handmade shoes out of the family home in Benito, Italy. In 1914, Ferragamo immigrated to Boston, where he briefly worked at a boot factory before moving to California and opening the Hollywood Boot Shop in 1923.

Ferragamo's made-to-measure shoes were a hit with movie stars, even after he returned to Italy in 1927. His shoes appeared in films ranging from *The Ten Commandments* (1956) to *Some Like It Hot* (1959). His designs for celebrities such as Lillian Gish, Rudolph Valentino, Mary Pickford, Douglas Fairbanks, Greta Garbo, Audrey Hepburn, Lauren Bacall, and Marilyn Monroe earned him the title "Shoemaker to the Stars."

Salvatore Ferragamo in his Florence workshop in
1956, with some of the lasts used to make shoes
for his celebrated clients.

Ferragamo was noted not only for his creative yet comfortable styles but also for his innovative use of materials, such as straw, raffia, cellophane, lace, and cork, and for his use of brilliant colors. Succinctly modern and yet consistently revivalist, Ferragamo was one of the first global names in twentieth-century Italian fashion.

Ferragamo's purple suede and gold metallic shoe with its wedge heel is an exquisite example of historical influence in fashion, evoking the chopines and the colorful banners of the Italian Renaissance.

Ankle Boots
ca. 1939
André Perugia, French, 1893–1977

The ankle boot was briefly revived in the years around 1939. Although not a mainstream style, it was included in the collections of numerous designers, including André Perugia and Elsa Schiaparelli. The elegant pair shown here is Perugia's modern interpretation of the side-buttoned ankle boot prevalent in the 1880s. His modern twist places the buttons toward the front rather than close to the ankle. Skillfully rendered crenellations appear at the top edges.

At a shoe factory in 1951, André Perugia looks through bins containing hundreds of lasts.

Pumps
1939

Attributed to André Perugia, French, 1893–1977,
for Elsa Schiaparelli, Italian, 1890–1973

This pair of custom-made shoes features a bold blue-and-black-
striped silk in alternating rib and satin weaves, an unusual fabric
choice that was almost certainly made to complement an ensemble by
Elsa Schiaparelli. Striped fabrics were featured in Schiaparelli's designs
for spring 1939, and the style-setting Standard Oil heiress, Millicent
Rogers, the original owner of these shoes, was an avid client.

Schiaparelli's shoes were made by André Perugia, and while
these shoes do not have the customary Perugia marks, the style and
superb workmanship suggest that he was responsible for their creation.

Elsa Schiaparelli created her famous shoe hats for her
fall/winter 1937–38 collection. The design was inspired
by a Salvador Dalí (Spanish, 1904–1989) drawing, which
in turn was inspired by a photograph of the Surrealist
artist wearing a high-heel shoe on his head.

Evening Shoes
1939

Steven Arpad, French (b. Hungary), 1904–1999,
for House of Balenciaga, French, founded 1937

This pair of extraordinary shoes appeared in the October 1939 issue of *Vogue* as a design for Cristóbal Balenciaga but is actually the work of Steven Arpad, who was Balenciaga's primary shoe designer in the late 1930s. Like that of many shoe designers, most of Arpad's work was done anonymously and released under the name of an established fashion house, so the 1939 archive of Arpad's shoe prototypes and sketches in The Costume Institute provides the sole documentation of this period in the designer's career.

In this fantastical footwear design, Arpad presents a unique rendition of the platform sole popular at the time. Although his source of inspiration is not documented, Arpad's black-lacquered supports strongly recall the Japanese *geta,* or wood clog.

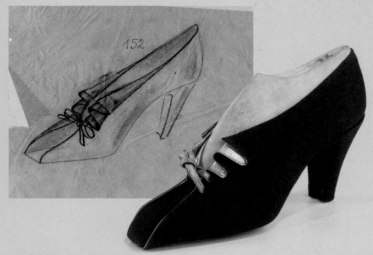

Model No. 152: The refinement of the design masks the simple concept of this model: a piece of leather brought up around the foot and tied at the throat, with the loose edges collapsing in graceful folds.

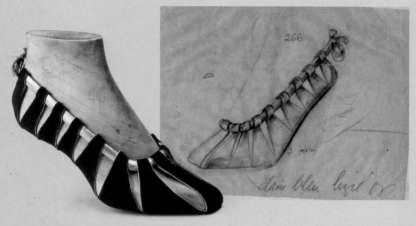

Model No. 266: With typical élan, Arpad refines the simple moccasin concept— leather drawn up from the bottom of the foot and held with a drawstring—into an elegant, sophisticated design.

Steven Arpad

French (b. Hungary), 1904–1999

S teven Arpad worked in Paris before World War II as the exclusive shoe designer for Cristóbal Balenciaga and for the American firms Delman and I. Miller. In 1947, encouraged by the great American couturier Charles James, Arpad donated more than seventy-five shoe prototypes that he had designed in 1939, along with an extensive archive of related drawings to the Brooklyn Museum Costume Collection, now at The Costume Institute. Known in the industry as "pullovers," the prototypes are models formed over and nailed to wood lasts, some with heels and some without. The drawings, which have made it possible to identify some of Arpad's anonymously created designs, document his creative process and his particular take on high-style couture shoe designs.

Model No. 463: Here, Arpad created a sculptural fantasy, where graduated prowlike flanges seem to swallow up the front of the foot.

Ankle Boots
1939

Steven Arpad, French (b. Hungary), 1904–1999,
for House of Balenciaga, French, founded 1937

Described in an October 1939 *Vogue* spread as "Balenciaga's back-fastened boot of brown antelope, the heel and platform of brown kid," these unlabeled suede ankle boots are undoubtedly the work of Steven Arpad.

Although the platform sole was an important design element in the late 1930s and 1940s, Arpad's unusual boots reference the seventeenth-century slap sole. Women's high-fashion slap-sole shoes evolved from the practice of men wearing flat-soled mules over high-heel riding boots so that their heels wouldn't sink into soft ground. Arpad's boots reference the original mule in the piping that crosses the vamp. However, unlike early slap-sole boots, which had a hinged sole that slapped against the heel as the wearer walked, Arpad's boots have soles that are attached to the heels.

Evening Shoes
1939

Steven Arpad, French (b. Hungary), 1904–1999

Famed manufacturer Herman Delman hired many of the most talented and creative designers of the 1930s, 1940s, and 1950s to create styles for his line of high-end women's shoes. The design of this unusual pair of patterned kid evening pumps incorporates Japanese and South Asian influences to whimsical yet superbly chic effect. Although not credited, the idiosyncratic design can be traced with some certainty to Steven Arpad, based on a sketch (top right) of an extremely similar model from 1939 in the Arpad archives at The Costume Institute.

Platform Sandals
ca. 1940

Victor, American

Many of the most innovative treatments of platform shoes were created between 1937 and 1942. In a direct reference to the chopines of the fifteenth to the seventeenth century, Victor, the designer of these red suede sandals, created an elegant high-style version of the platform. The graceful curving shape of the undercut heel provides the sandals with a dramatic focal point.

Platform Sandals
ca. 1943

American

An updated version of the platform shoe emerged in the second half of the 1930s as a counterpart to the wedge heel. While the wedge had waned by the mid-1940s, high-heel platforms remained in fashion for several more years. With its exaggeratedly high heels, this pair of suede platforms with metallic gold piping from Penét Shoes, Inc., is an extreme example of the style. The tied ankle strap is a fashion echo of the headscarves often worn by women factory workers of the time.

Opposite page:
Dancer/actress Carmen Miranda was famous for her outlandish hats and high platform shoes. Here, she's shown in 1944 with part of her large shoe collection, which included both wedge and high-heel platforms.

"Invisible" Sandals
1947

Salvatore Ferragamo, Italian, 1898–1960

Semitransparent elements are a notable feature of Salvatore Ferragamo's mature work. In his iconic "Invisible" sandal, a continuous length of nylon monofilament passes back and forth through holes in the insole to create the upper. Originally, a buckled leather strap fastened at the front of the ankle, but it has deteriorated in this example. The use of metallic leather helps to dematerialize the remaining structure of the shoe. Ferragamo called his elegant undercut wedge the F-heel.

In the "Luito" shoe, a lesser-known version of Ferragamo's "Invisible" sandal, the nylon thread passes through a neutral-colored binding, retaining a minimal structure on the otherwise dematerialized upper.

In 1954, Jasper Johns (American, b. 1930) began the first of his American flag images. Though *Flag* resembles its model, the static, highly textured painting calls attention to the difference between a physical work and what it portrays. In a patriotic era, this ambiguity raised the question of whether the painting was, as one art critic put it, respectful or blasphemous.

Platform Sandals
ca. 1950

Dominick LaValle, American

A merica's emergence in the post–World War II period as the wealthiest and most powerful nation in the world was reflected in a surge of patriotic imagery, most popularly the Stars and Stripes. While the flag itself was handled with veneration—it had to be folded in a particular way and couldn't be allowed to touch the ground— its graphic components as well as its colors appeared everywhere, including on clothing.

An example is Dominick LaValle's set of red, white, and blue accessories. In addition to the platform sandals, he designed a star-studded clutch with matching coin purse and mirror, and mid-arm-length white gloves with gauntlet-style red-and-blue cuffs also studded with stars.

Marabou Mules
1950–59

American

Perhaps no object better epitomizes the sex-kitten glamour of the 1950s than the marabou mule. The style has become an icon of feminine allure, making it the only significant modern survivor of the boudoir slipper. The transparent acrylic sole of the mules shown here increases the iconic potency of the design by making reference to Cinderella, the unrivaled superstar of shoe lore. Adding to their glamorous aura, these mules belonged to actress Joan Fontaine.

In this scene from *The Seven Year Itch* (1955), Marilyn Monroe wears a fur-trimmed negligee and marabou mules.

Together and separately, the DeMarcos appeared in several films, most notably for Ms. DeMarco, *Gone with the Wind* (1939), in which she played Vivien Leigh in all the dance shots that were not close-ups.

Dance Shoes
1951

American

In 1962, Tony and Sally DeMarco, a prominent professional ballroom dance team in the 1940s, donated garments and shoes to the Brooklyn Museum Costume Collection, now at The Costume Institute. Most of these were associated with the DeMarcos' professional activities. Although Mr. DeMarco's footwear was made specifically for dancing, Ms. DeMarco's shoes are standard Palter DeLiso evening sandals, with a rubber tread added for traction. With its interesting asymmetric design and contrasting textures and colors, this pair of sandals is unique among the group, as the others are satin sandals in two styles (closed and open back) dyed in a rainbow of colors to match Ms. DeMarco's gowns.

Shoes
1952

Hubert de Givenchy, French, b. 1927

T he early work of designers tends to be scarce as they have not yet built the reputation and significant following necessary to assure preservation of their work. When an early piece does survive, it is often highly prized for its capacity to illustrate the young talent's freshness and unfettered spirit, qualities that are difficult to maintain throughout a career.

Unusual for both its material and toe treatment, this deep-pink straw shoe was created the year after Givenchy opened his couture house. The design is playful but sophisticated, and as Givenchy was known for chic and monochromatic designs that focused on line rather than decoration, it fits easily into his aesthetic. The shoe was probably made by André Perugia, who was known to execute Givenchy's footwear at the time.

Hubert de Givenchy poses with columnist Cobina Wright and actress Sara Shane at the Hollywood premiere of the film *So Big* (1953).

Stocking Shoes
1953

Beth Levine, American, 1914–2006

Top American shoe designer Beth Levine, wife of manufacturer Herbert Levine, was particularly adept at predicting future trends and devising structural innovations. Preserved in her personal collection, this is the first version of Levine's original stocking shoe design, which she repeated in various forms beginning in the mid-1950s and continuing through the late 1960s. Later examples included pantyhose tops.

Extremely avant-garde for the early 1950s, Beth Levine's stocking shoes were considered risqué when they were introduced.

Sandal
1954–58

Italian

One of the approximately 175 examples of footwear collected in Europe by Charline Osgood, director of the Kid Leather Guild, this masterful variation on the sandal shows what Osgood called "Modern Functionalism" in design. The materials are used in a way that expresses their natural beauty: the design is very simple, clean, and modern-looking, and the form, with the extended ends of the sole curving up to cradle the foot, is logical and organic.

Osgood collected the items, mostly fashionable Italian-made women's shoes, in the mid-1950s to show American manufacturers the creative possibilities fine kid leather offered for use in footwear.

Shoe
1954–58

Enzo Albanese, Italian, 1933–2003

lbanese of Roma was founded in 1925 by Armando Albanese and became prominent during World War II. His son, Enzo, joined the company in 1951 and soon raised the quality and originality of the brand to the couture level. Film stars such as Sophia Loren, Raquel Welsh, and Anita Ekberg were clients of the firm.

The deep-red suede shoe at right is a close copy of a latchet shoe from the late seventeenth or early eighteenth century, superbly executed with modern methods and materials. Although not widespread, upturned pointed toes, high tongues, and Louis heels do appear on other models from the 1950s, although seldom with such blatant historicism.

The period inspiration for Albanese's shoe can be seen in the embroidered latchet shoe above from about 1700. Despite its poor condition, it is an excellent example of the era's high-style women's shoes.

Sandals
1955

Mario Valentino, Italian, 1927–1991

After working with his father, the noted shoemaker Vincenzo Valentino, Mario Valentino opened his own company in 1952 in Naples, where it is still headquartered today. Over the years, Valentino clients have included Jacqueline Kennedy Onassis, Maria Callas, Elizabeth Taylor, and Catherine Deneuve.

The pair of sandals shown here was designed with a matching pair of gloves, with the aim of promoting both the use of kid and the coordination of gloves and shoes among American manufacturers. Charline Osgood, then director of the Kid Leather Guild, a trade organization of American kid leather manufacturers, noted that Valentino's design would be particularly appropriate for the American market in different heel heights.

In this characteristically ironic version of Beth Levine's topless shoe, the wearer would appear to be standing barefoot in the forest.

Topless Shoes
1955–60

Beth Levine, American, 1914–2006

Beth Levine's unique design reduces footwear to its most essential element—the sole—and treats it as a decorative abstract shape. While her topless shoes were in fact functional (they were secured to the foot with adhesive pads), they were more important as a theoretical exercise than a significant fashion. Levine garnered praise early in her career by producing flatteringly sexy, low-cut, and flesh-baring footwear and later produced a wide assortment of shoes with transparent vinyl uppers and/or Lucite heels. The topless shoe was the absurdist culmination of that exploration.

Beth Levine

American, 1914–2006

Born in Patchogue, New York, Beth Katz moved from the family dairy farm to Manhattan in the 1930s. With her perfect sample-size 4B feet, she took a job as a shoe model and worked her way up to being head designer for I. Miller. She married Herbert Levine (1916–1991) in 1946, and in 1949 they opened a shoemaking company, with Beth designing and Herbert handling the business end and lending his name to the company.

Levine's ingenious and witty designs were sought by Hollywood stars such as Marilyn Monroe, Angela Lansbury, Barbara Streisand, Liza Minelli, and Cher, and her creations for Jacqueline Kennedy, Lady Bird Johnson, and Patricia Nixon earned her the sobriquet "America's First Lady of Shoe Design." Halston, Geoffrey Beene, and James Galanos were among the couturiers for whom she designed.

Beth Levine experimented with making shoes out of paper, including this pair of low-heeled sandals with ribbonlike strips of glossy orange reversing to yellow flocking.

Always a pacesetter, Levine figured out a way to attach Lucite heels without nails and was an early proponent of the spring-o-lator mule, which had an elastic strip along the insole that kept the backless shoe from slipping off or slapping against the wearer's heel when she walked. Levine is also known for her use of unusual materials such as paper, rhinestone pavé, and AstroTurf. For their boundary-breaking innovations, the Levines received Coty American Fashion Critics' Awards in 1967 and 1973.

Sandal
ca. 1958

Enzo Albanese, Italian, 1933–2003

I talian shoe designers experimented with many variations of the slender stiletto heel in the later 1950s. As the height and thinness of the heel increased, an internal steel shank was introduced to prevent breakage, inspiring inventive designers to dispose of the outer material altogether and create models with spindly metal heels. Italian heels of this period were often set well under the foot to provide stability, and though the architectural cant of the bladelike heel on this sandal from Albanese of Roma looks odd, it is a structural necessity.

Cocktail Shoes
ca. 1958

David Evins, American (b. England), 1909–1991

Dubbed the "King of Pumps" and the "Dean of American Shoe Designers," David Evins is remembered for his elegant but comfortable shoes. He designed for a "who's who" of movie stars, including Ava Gardner, Judy Garland, and Marlene Dietrich, as well as for First Ladies from Mamie Eisenhower to Nancy Reagan. While Evins's work is often geared to a classic and conservative taste, the detailing is always exacting and sometimes unexpected.

The basic form of the pair of shoes shown here is a classic stiletto pump, refined in shape and remarkable for its superb craftsmanship. The ornamentation, while subtle, is highly effective and innovative in its placement and fabrication.

For her wedding to Prince Rainier of Monaco on April 19, 1956, Grace Kelly wore shoes designed by David Evins.

Sandals
1958

Domenico Albion, Italian

The use of red, blue, and yellow suede and kid is playful in this appealing pair of slingback sandals. The detailed sock lining shows the high level of craftsmanship of the better Italian makers and, from other examples, seems to have been a hallmark of designer Domenico Albion. The style illustrates the Spanish and Flamenco influence on 1950s fashion as well as the contemporary trends of ornamental lining and looped straps.

Sandal
1958

Alberto Dal Co', Italian, 1902–1963

C harline Osgood, director of the Kid Leather Guild in the 1950s, considered this sandal by Albert Dal Co' to be one of the most exciting and radical designs in her shoe collection, now in the Brooklyn Museum Costume Collection at The Costume Institute. The toe of the T-strap is unique, ostensibly inspired by Japanese *tabi,* socks that have a separation between the big toe and the other toes so that they can be worn with thongs. And true to Osgood's assertions as to the anatomical sensitivity of Italian shoe design, the T-strap follows the line of the first metatarsal bone.

A young woman wearing thongs and *tabi* reaches up to steady a branch in this detail from *Picking Persimmons*, a woodblock print by Kitagawa Utamaro (Japanese, 1753/54–1806).

Cocktail Shoes
1958

Alberto Dal Co', Italian, 1902–1963

S hortly after World War II ended, Alberto Dal Co', a young shoemaker from Traversetolo, moved to Rome, where he founded his own business, specializing in custom-made shoes. Although Dal Co' is not well known today, his inventiveness and superb craftsmanship place him in the top tier of masters of his trade. Gina Lollobrigida, Sophia Loren, Audrey Hepburn, Ava Gardner, and Diana Vreeland were just a few of his famous clients.

The superb line and unique heel treatment of this elegant pair of shoes are typical Dal Co' work. While the peaked toe was a popular style in Italy, it never caught on in the United States.

Shoe
1958

Alberto Dal Co', Italian, 1902–1963

While this inventive casual shoe by Alberto Dal Co' may bring a court jester to mind, the long, turned-up toe with its tiny brass bead at the end is clearly derived from traditional Indo-Pakistani footwear. The functionalist single-seam construction and amusing but expertly engineered heel with its two small cylinders resembling wheels are of particular interest.

Evening Shoe
1958

Beth Levine, American, 1914–2006

The beauty of peacock feathers has made their use a perennial motif in fashion. In 1903, Lady Curzon, wife of the viceroy to India, referenced the country's royal associations with the bird in the dress she wore to the State Ball of the Delhi Durbar, where King Edward VII was proclaimed Emperor of India. In the 1949 film *Samson and Delilah,* Hedy Lamarr wore a peacock-feather cape designed by Edith Head. Rudi Gernreich created a peacock-print minidress with matching stockings and a peacock-tail-feather headdress in 1966, and in 2007, Alexander McQueen designed a dress with a peacock-feather bustier (left).

Here, Beth Levine completely covered a pump with peacock feathers. Adorned with a sparkling piece of Jean Schlumberger jewelry, the style was featured in a window at Tiffany & Company in New York in 1958.

Boots
1959

Beth Levine, American, 1914–2006

As hemlines began to rise again in the late 1950s, so did the uppers of boots, as can be seen in this knee-high pair designed by Beth Levine for the Herbert Levine company. The use of the Dalmatian print stenciled on the outer side of the boots (the inner side is black glacé calf) reflects Levine's wittiness as well as the increasing vogue for less expensive "fun fur," which was launched in the second half of the 1950s by furrier Jacques Kaplan.

Pump
Late 1950s–early 1960s

Mabel Julianelli, American, 1909–1994

After studying commercial art at the Pratt Institute, Mabel Julianelli began her career as a pattern designer in Brooklyn. In the 1930s, she and her husband, Charles, started their own shoe business and became known for their comfortable yet stylish shoes. Julianelli was also known for setting trends. For example, she designed sandals for fall, ignoring "the rule that bare shoes come out only in spring and winter," as fashion writer Angela Taylor commented in a *New York Times* article in 1964. The spare, elegant contours of the classic Julianelli pump shown here are enhanced by lines of sequins and beads that follow the shape of the shoe.

Mabel Julianelli introduced the "Naked" evening sandal in 1949, when sandals were practically unheard of for evening wear. The following year, she and her husband were awarded a Coty American Fashion Critics' Award for artistry and craftsmanship.

Evening Shoes
ca. 1960

Italian

As stilettos developed over the second half of the 1950s and the early 1960s, sharp, elongated, angular lines became increasingly important. The slender, linear effect in this pair of black silk pumps, manufactured in Italy by Raphael, is complemented by the acute angle of the toe slanting up from the sole, the low cut of the upper, and the skeletal cut-out ornament. The beadwork adds a lively and luxurious effect to the severe lines while maintaining the linear theme.

Evening Shoes
1960

Roger Vivier, French, 1913–1998, for House of Dior, French, founded 1947

In 1955, Roger Vivier created two new heel designs for Christian Dior: the *talon choc* ("shock heel") and the *talon aiguille* ("needle heel"). Both shoes shown here are examples of the talon choc, which gives the back of each shoe its distinctive convex curve. This curve is echoed in the topline of one side of each shoe, while on the opposite side, the topline curves gracefully down to create a concave silhouette. The concave curve on the purple and turquoise satin shoe is punctuated with a matching two-tone bow. The other shoe is black satin covered with iridescent hummingbird feathers from the tip of the heel to the tip of the very pointed toe.

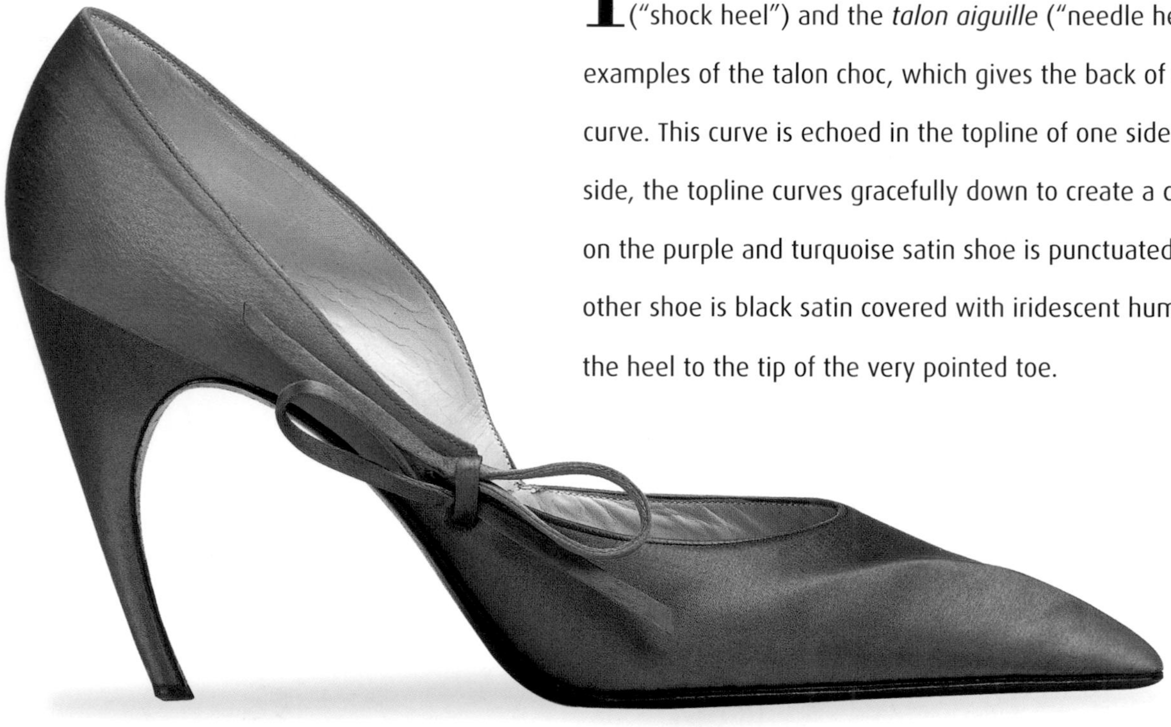

Evening Shoes
1961

Roger Vivier, French, 1913–1998, for House of Dior, French, founded 1947

The shoe designer for Christian Dior from the 1940s to the 1960s, Roger Vivier was known for his exquisite forms and extravagant materials. Both are evident in this evening pump with its comma heel and elaborate embroidery of glass beads, rhinestones, and silver metallic thread on aqua satin. By adding an upturned toe and using the turquoise blue associated with the glazes and semiprecious stones of the Middle East, Vivier created his own fabulous version of the Orientalist slipper. This kind of extravagant decoration often adorned Vivier's elegant feminine shoes, and he became known as the "Fabergé of Footwear."

Roger Vivier

French, 1913–1998

For more than sixty years, Roger Vivier designed women's shoes, creating footwear for François Pinet, Rayne and Turner, Elsa Schiaparelli, Herbert Delman, Madame Grès, Cristóbal Balenciaga, and Yves Saint Laurent, among others. Vivier was noted for his feminine, often extravagantly ornamented shoes, such as the evening boot from 1957 below.

In 1953, Vivier designed Queen Elizabeth's coronation shoes, a pair of gold kid high-heel sandals studded with garnets. That same year, he began creating shoes exclusively for Christian Dior and became the first shoe designer to share label credit with a couturier. In 1963, Vivier left Dior to open his own atelier in Paris.

Vivier was among the first—some say *the* first—to design stiletto heels, which he originally made to complement the hourglass shape of Dior's "New Look" collections. Vivier's interest in sculpture (he studied at the École des Beaux-Arts in the 1920s) led him to experiment with heel silhouettes, and he developed the comma heel with aeronautical engineers, the *talon choc* heel, with its concave structure, and the thorn heel, which featured the shape of a rose thorn protruding from the back.

Mule, 1962
Slingback Shoe, ca. 1962

Beth Levine, American, 1914–2006

Beth Levine's creative genius is evidenced in the unusual rolled heels on the turquoise velvet and silver kid mule at left and the tan calf slingback below. In addition to the rolled heel, Levine produced another shoe in the same vein, where instead of rolling the leather, she used accordion folds to form a cube.

Evening Boots
ca. 1962

Beth Levine, American, 1914–2006

Beth Levine is credited with resurrecting high-fashion boots in the early 1960s. She later said in a *Boston Globe* article, "Boots moved into prominence the same time The Pill did. Both were symbols of a woman's new freedom and emancipation."

While presaging the flat go-go boots that André Courrèges introduced with his space-age ensembles of 1964, these boots are a transitional style incorporating the fashionable stiletto heel. The metallic brocaded fabric and applied rhinestones reflect the high-style fashion of the time, when evening dresses were typically encrusted with beads.

In 1966, Nancy Sinatra wore boots by Beth Levine while performing her #1 hit "These Boots Are Made for Walkin'" by singer/songwriter Lee Hazlewood. Though Levine had moved closer to the go-go boot style, she still retained the stiletto heel.

Slippers
1964–65

Emilio Pucci, Italian, 1914–1992

The son of a wealthy aristocrat, Marchese Emilio Pucci di Barsento was an Olympic skier and won a skiing scholarship to Reed College in Oregon, where he designed sportswear for his team. His fashion career was launched in 1947 when an editor at *Harper's Bazaar* saw photographs of a ski outfit Pucci had designed and invited him to create clothes for an article on winter fashion.

Pucci opened a shop in Capri in 1950 and presented his first line of couture designs, featuring the bright colors and bold prints for which he would become famous. These gold kid slippers, with their elongated turned-up toe and teardrop pearl, were worn with free-flowing lounging pajamas (left) at Pucci's fashion show in 1964.

"Kick Off" Shoes
ca. 1965

Beth Levine, American, 1914–2006

Noted for her creative design, structural innovations, and experimentation with novel materials, Beth Levine is considered by many to be the top female shoe designer of the twentieth century. In the mid-1960s, Levine turned to sports for inspiration. Among the whimsical shoes she designed were a low-heeled white oxford, with red stitching adapted from a baseball, and the "Kick Off" shoes, with stitching and lacing adapted from a football, shown here.

"Kabuki" Evening Shoe
ca. 1965

Beth Levine, American, 1914–2006

Beth Levine's "Kabuki" line was inspired by traditional Asian footwear, borrowing its inspiration primarily from Manchu platform shoes. The line included pump and mule styles in a variety of satin fabrics, metallic leathers, and Persian lamb, with gilt or lacquered wood soles. In the pump at left, the gold-patterned silk upper complements the gilt sole. Designed to give the illusion that they are floating above their platforms, "Kabuki" shoes were often praised for their aerodynamic feeling.

The black satin upper of this 1962 version of Beth Levine's "Kabuki" shoe is studded with rhinestones, while the shaped wood sole is lacquered in black.

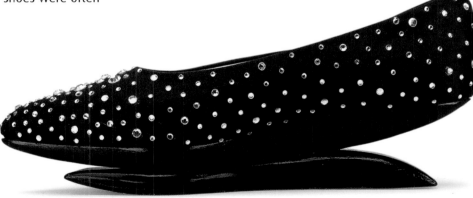

Slingback Shoes
1965

Charles Jourdan, French, 1883–1976

In 1919, Charles Jourdan founded his shoe business in Romans, France. Gradually, he built it into a premiere French luxury shoe manufacturer of both his own designs and those of numerous other top designers, including Christian Dior and Pierre Cardin. In 1957, Jourdan opened a boutique in Paris and by the 1960s had reached the height of his success. He became particularly known for offering a limited number of models in an extensive range of colors. Expressing the colorful Pop Art aesthetic of the 1960s, this pair of bright yellow slingback shoes features a playful rounded heel that echoes the center of the flower on the vamp.

Racing Car Shoes
1965–67

Katharina Denzinger, American

T he freewheeling creativity of Pop Art and the increasingly common use of plastics for footwear in the 1960s allowed free rein to Katharina Denzinger's imagination when she designed these shoes for a *Harper's Bazaar* editorial spread. Made of clear, colored, and mirrored vinyl shapes and trimmed with molded plastic "headlights," the shoes are designed to look like race cars, complete with numeric designation and "windshields." The shoes were executed by the Herbert Levine company. In 1967, Beth Levine created her own race-car design for the wife of an Indianapolis 500 driver.

Shoes
1965–75

David Evins, American (b. England), 1909–1991

The fashionable owner of these shoes by David Evins paired them with a handbag (left) by Lucille de Paris, a New York–based company that specialized in the use of alligator and other exotic skins. Matching handbag and shoes were de rigueur for the well-dressed woman in the mid-twentieth century, but because shoes were prone to wearing faster, they were often discarded before the bag, making intact sets relatively rare. Both the handbag and the shoes in this conservative but high-quality pairing are made of alligator leather, and the shoes feature gold studs and metallic kid piping on the wide tabs.

Boots

ca. 1967

André Courrèges, French, b. 1923

T o complement his avant-garde clothing, André Courrèges offered equally innovative shoes. While the starkly tailored Courrèges boot has become an icon of his space-age look, this slightly later pair takes a softer form. His designs avoided the darker potentialities of a technology-based future, concentrating instead on a Utopian world of playful and childlike sweetness. The detailing of the boots closely follows that of Courrèges's double-faced wool garments, with raised welt seams, round-ended tabs, and concealed closures.

Opposite page:
André Courrèges (third from left) poses with his models in 1968. The female model standing next to him wears boots similar to those shown at right.

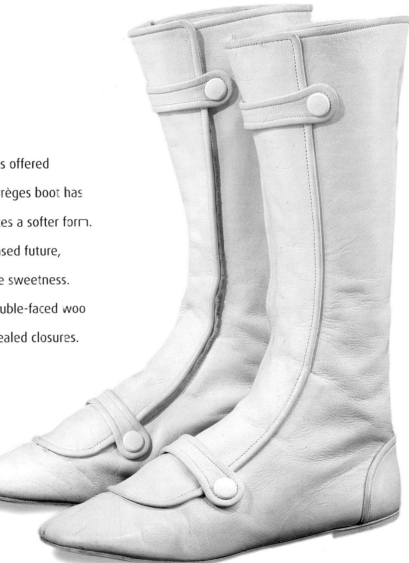

Ankle Boots
1967

Pierre Cardin, French, b. 1922

I n the 1960s, designers were incorporating plastics, Velcro, and high-tech fibers into their shoes. These new materials seemed ideally suited to clothing and footwear in the era of space-age technology, but they often blurred the line between utilitarian or athletic styles and high fashion.

Pierre Cardin's black patent-leather ankle boots, part of an ensemble that included a white turtleneck sweater and black double-knit tunic and trousers, have a zipper closure, a feature not commonly seen in footwear prior to the 1960s. The large circles on the sides are evocative of the 45-rpm vinyl record single, whose popularity began to wane in the late 1960s as albums with multiple songs became more prevalent.

Boots
Late 1960s

Roger Vivier, French, 1913–1998

T high-high boots had been worn as fetish footwear, but they didn't become a fashion trend until the 1960s, when Roger Vivier began designing them for celebrities. Among his creations was a pair of black leather boots for Brigitte Bardot, who wore them while sitting on a Harley-Davidson motorcycle in a film clip, and a pair of crocodile-skin boots for Rudolf Nureyev.

The knee-length boots shown here may look like dyed snakeskin but, in fact, they're red and black patterned plastic. The boots were owned by Diana Vreeland, who at various times was a columnist at *Harper's Bazaar,* editor in chief of *Vogue,* and consultant to The Costume Institute.

Diana Vreeland, photographed here by Jonathan Becker, loved the color red (the walls and floors of her apartment were covered in it)—and shoes. Roger Vivier was one of her favorite footwear designers.

Platform Shoes
ca. 1973

Brazilian (left)
American (right)

I n 1967, the historicizing hippie look overtook fashion, spurring the revival of the platform sole, which had enjoyed wide success in the 1940s. Before long, designers were making modern versions with exaggerated bulgy toes, flaring heels, and curvaceous soles. Colorful piecing and patchwork were frequently used to add a fresh, graphic quality to the uppers.

Many of the best examples of the era's platform shoe come from Latin America, where the style was particularly favored. In the example at left, made by Dasaje do Brasil, the visual impact is intensified by bold colors and the treatment of the upper and sole as a continuous unit. Though more subdued in the example on the right, made by the Mary Poppins company, the two-tone color scheme emphasizes the height of the platform, while the dark stitching on the vamp calls attention to the geometric pattern.

Pumps
ca. 1974

Vivienne Westwood, British, b. 1941

In 1971, Vivienne Westwood and her partner, Malcolm McLaren, opened their London store, Let It Rock. Three years later, they changed the store's name to SEX, decorated the walls with pornographic graffiti, and began selling S&M-inspired clothes. The shop became the center of the Punk fashion scene, and McLaren and Westwood (at right in 1981) are often credited with creating the dynamic relationship between music and fashion that set the tone of popular culture for decades to come.

The rubber-soled red stiletto pump shown here bears the label "SEX/430 Kings Rd./Chelsea" and was featured in a 1994 painting by artist Luciana Martinez de la Rosa (British, 1948–1995) called *Sex—The Red Shoes.*

Boots
ca. 1975
American

hen boots, which had slipped out of fashion in the 1920s, returned as an important style in the early 1960s, they had a modernistic feeling, like the go-go boots by André Courrèges. By the late 1960s, however, the bohemian influence on fashion was generating boots that harked back to their historical predecessors. These high lace-up boots became known as granny boots.

The pair shown here is enlivened by colorful folk-style embroidery that brings to mind the expression "Flower Power," coined in 1965 by poet Allen Ginsberg (American, 1926–1997). The boots bear the label "From the Greek Workshops of Jerry Edouard," which is thought to be a pseudonym used by shoe retailer E. Jerrold (Jerry) Miller, grandson of the founder of I. Miller Shoe Company. Miller was known to have imported shoes from Greece in the 1970s.

Evening Sandals
1980

Hubert de Givenchy, French, b. 1927

A fter the heavy styles of the later 1960s and the 1970s, shoe fashion was overdue for a shift to a lighter, more delicate aesthetic. Glamorous evening sandals in a rainbow of glittery colors with slender straps and high spike heels perfectly complemented the sexy disco-style fashions of the late 1970s and early 1980s This pair by Hubert de Givenchy epitomizes the type. Sequins, which produce a lively sparkle with minimum weight, are perfect for crawing attention to a dancer's flashing feet.

Boots
1980s

Maud Frizon, French, b. 1941

Maud Frizon began her career as a fashion model in 1958. Nine years later, she met Luigi de Marco while modeling his shoes in a salon, and in 1969, the two launched their first collection, featuring a zipper-free high Russian boot with a fold-down top. Frizon's shoes were an immediate success, and she opened her first shop in Paris that same year. In addition to creating under her own name, Frizon has designed for Missoni, Sonia Rykiel, Thierry Mugler, and other couturiers. These geometrically pieced suede boots with their modified pyramid heel bear Frizon's trademark bold colors.

Pumps
ca. 1985

Susan Bennis/Warren Edwards, American, 1977–97

The Bennis/Edwards partnership began in 1972, when they started a dress business. Next, they opened a small store in New York to sell Chelsea Cobbler shoes along with their clothes. By 1980, they had moved to Park Avenue and were designing their own shoes under the name Susan Bennis/Warren Edwards.

Bennis/Edwards shoes were distinctive not only for their high price tags but also for their styling. The partners used exotic skins in bold colors and covered evening shoes with beads and rhinestones. Some of their shoes even evidenced a sly sense of humor, such their Birkenstock-like evening sandals with rhinestone buckles and the pumps evocative of comic books and Pop Art shown here. The black suede is embellished with leather appliqués featuring the words *pop, pow,* and *power* in splotches of bright orange and pink.

Pumps
ca. 1986

Tokio Kumagaï, Japanese, 1948–1987

After working for fashion designers Jean-Charles de Castelbajac and Nino Cerruti, Tokio Kumagaï opened his own Paris boutique in 1980. He began hand-painting shoes in 1979, using the shoe as a canvas for surrealistic designs based on the work of artists such as Salvador Dalí (Spanish, 1904–1989), Piet Mondrian (Dutch, 1872–1944), and Wassily Kandinsky (French, b. Russia, 1866–1944).

Kumagaï's more whimsical designs included faces on the vamp. The cat design at left is the counterpart of Kumagaï's most famous creation, the mouse design at right.

In René Magritte's *The Great Family* (1963), puffy white clouds and a sunlit sky take the form of a dove in a stormy seascape.

Pumps
1986

Armando Pollini, Italian

Surrealist artists sought to create unexpected, surprising imagery by liberating the subconscious imagination. Among the best-known Surrealists are René Magritte (Belgian, 1898–1967) and Salvador Dalí (Spanish, 1904–1989). Their works, often realistically painted but with a dreamlike quality, challenge the viewers' notions of reality. Though the organized Surrealist movement dissolved with the onset of World War II, the imagery of Surrealism has persisted to the present day.

Perhaps Armando Pollini was alluding to a Magritte painting when he created these shoes dotted with puffy clouds against a bright blue "sky." Or perhaps he simply wanted to lift the wearer's spirits and make her feel as if she were walking on clouds.

"Goya" Shoes
1986–87

Roger Vivier, French, 1913–1998

The perforated leather and scalloped topline of Roger Vivier's "Goya" shoes are like a magnified view of the edge of a black lace mantilla. The shoes are extraordinary not only for Vivier's elegant comma heel, here in gold-tone metal, but also for the craftsmanship required to make them. The shoes are composed of patent leather cut out in a beehive pattern, wrapped with black silk thread, and reinforced on the inside with narrow strips of metallic gold leather. The handwork for each pair of shoes took thirty hours, and they were produced in a limited quantity by the Italian firm René Caovilla and sold exclusively at Vivier's Madison Avenue shop, then the only one in the world.

Pumps
1988–89

Isabel Canovas, French, b. 1945

The daughter of a textile designer who worked with Cristóbal Balenciaga, accessories designer Isabel Canovas never formally studied design. After spending seven years at the House of Dior learning her craft, Canovas opened her first shop in Paris in 1982. Her collections showcased accessories designed with witty imaginative touches. Shown here are two examples: hot-pink satin pumps (1988) crawling with ants made out of glittering black sequins and a surrealistic flat (1989) that could pass for a half-peeled ripe banana.

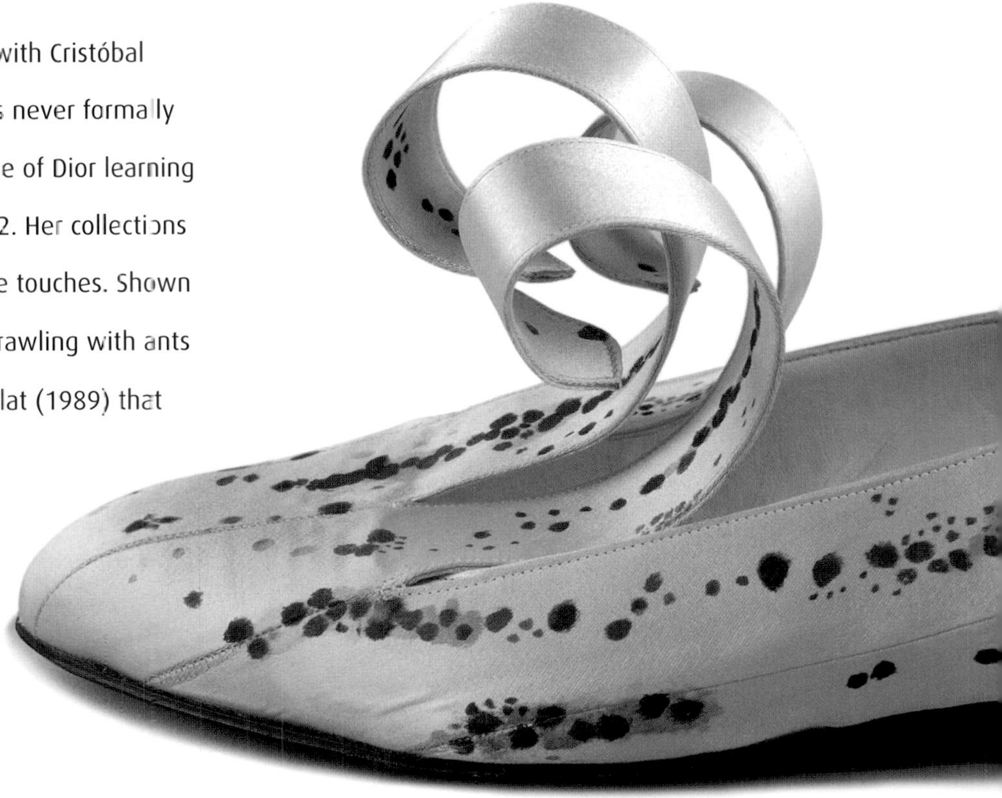

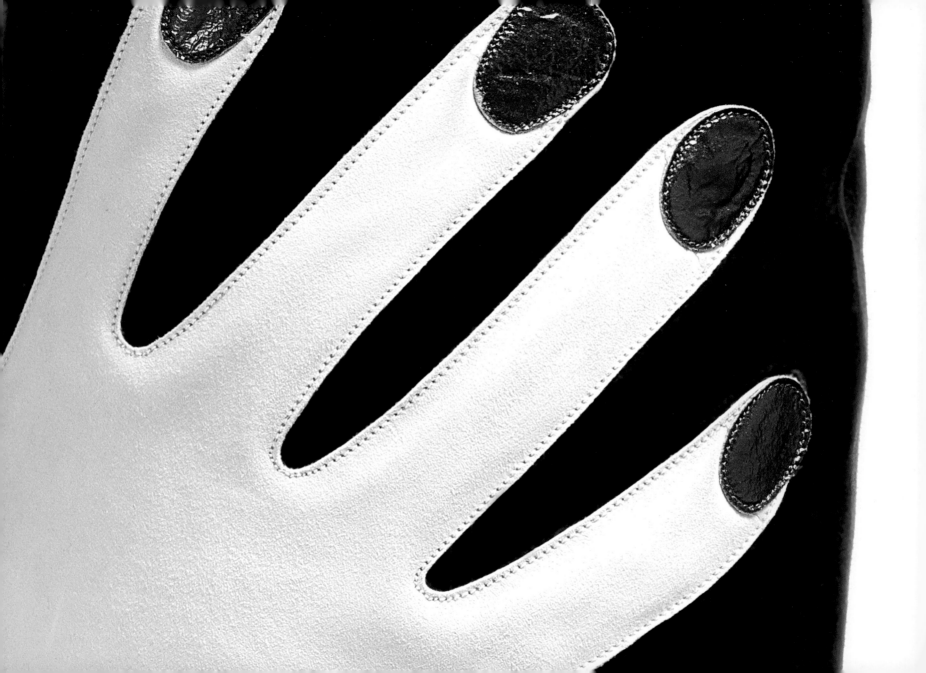

Boots
ca. 1990

Andrea Pfister, French (b. Italy), b. 1942

A ndrea Pfister designed shoes for the couture houses of Jeanne Lanvin and Jean Patou before opening his first Paris shop in 1967. Since then, his often colorful, well-made shoes have graced the feet of many celebrities, including Claudia Cardinale, Candice Bergen, and Liza Minelli.

Pfister has said his shoes are "full of humor," and his creations often exhibit an air of lightheartedness. Examples include his "Martini Dry" pump featuring a heel shaped like a cocktail glass with a slice of lemon at the top and his "Capri" thong sandal decorated with an open parasol on the strap and bright red nails on the toe of the metallic gold insole. Red nails appear again on the slip-on knee-high boots shown here, this time adorning ghost-white hands appliquéd on the soft black suede.

"Portrait" Shoes
1990

Vivienne Westwood, British, b. 1941

Since the 1970s, Vivienne Westwood has gone from Punk fashion trendsetter to Dame Commander of the Order of the British Empire, given for services to British fashion. Along the way, she's moved from Punk and S&M fashion to her historicizing Pagan and Anglomania lines to her current Exploration collections. Today, Westwood is considered one of the most influential fashion designers of the twentieth century.

In the 1990s, Westwood revisited the platform heels popular in the 1930s, 1940s, and 1970s, taking them to new heights. The hot-pink patent-leather platform pumps shown here were created for her "Portrait" collection.

In 1993, model Naomi Campbell, known for her assurance and agility on the runway, tripped while walking in a pair of eight-inch-high Vivienne Westwood platforms.

Evening Shoes
1990–92

Manolo Blahnik, British (b. Spain), b. 1942

Manolo Blahnik has reached truly iconic status as a shoe designer and is one of the few whose name has become synonymous with his footwear. He began designing in the early 1970s and by the 1980s, was producing some of the most sought-after shoes in the world. Princess Diana, Jacqueline Kennedy Onassis, Lauren Bacall, and Madonna (who once said Blahnik's shoes were "as good as sex") have numbered among his clients.

Often compared to Roger Vivier, Blahnik is renowned for the artistry, delicacy, and allure of his designs. In 1990 and 1999, he was named Accessory Designer of the Year by the British Fashion Council and in 2007 was awarded an honorary CBE (Commander of the British Empire) "in recognition of his status as one of the most successful and influential designers of our time."

The pair of slate-blue satin and violet suede pumps shown here features a needle toe, a high heel, and romantic historicizing design exemplified by the faux latchet closure across the high tongue and the buckle decorated with rhinestones.

Manolo Blahnik

British (b. Spain), b. 1942

Even before Sarah Jessica Parker as Carrie Bradshaw in *Sex and the City* made "Manolos" a household name, Manolo Blahnik was famous among fashion aficionados for his elegant and sexy shoes. Yet, surprisingly, his entry into shoe design came about by chance. In 1971, while Blahnik was visiting New York, a friend arranged for him to meet Diana Vreeland, then editor in chief of *Vogue.* When she saw the drawings in his portfolio, Vreeland thought the accessories—especially the shoes—were amusing and said, "Go make shoes." Blahnik did.

Blahnik's designs quickly gained popularity with fashion editors and young celebrities. In 1973, he bought Zapata, a London boutique frequented by Bianca Jagger, and in 1979, opened his first New York store. Today, Blahnik continues to personally create all the designs and prototypes for his shoes, making the sketches, carving the wood lasts on which they're molded, and sculpting the heels.

Reminiscent of a fashionable eighteenth-century style, this romantic mule exemplifies Manolo Blahnik's ultrafeminine look.

"Thorn" Evening Sandals
1993

Roger Vivier, French, 1913–1998

Roger Vivier's first connection with the Delman company was in the 1940s and early 1950s. In fact, he was still under contract to Delman in his first years with the House of Dior, as the shoe labels attest. In 1992, Vivier, one of the most revered shoe designers of the twentieth century, renewed his relationship with Delman and began revisiting many of his iconic features, such as the thorn heel. In this pair of black crêpe evening sandals, the point of the thorn is echoed in the peaked throat and gold-tone metal buckle.

Boots
1993–94

**Karl Lagerfeld, French (b. Germany), b. 1938,
for House of Chanel, French, founded 1913**

A decade after the death of Gabrielle "Coco" Chanel, the House of Chanel was still respected as the epitome of classic French taste but had become somewhat senescent. That changed with the appointment of Karl Lagerfeld (left) as its creative director in 1984.

Lagerfeld's fabled sense of the moment and rich cultural knowledge quickly animated the house. Faithful to the irreverent attitude of the pre–World War II Chanel, a savvy outsider who flaunted convention and turned taste on its head, Lagerfeld used his understanding of Chanel's aesthetic vocabulary to exaggerate the small details and nuances of her style with a bold contemporary exuberance.

In the boots shown here, Lagerfeld exploited many "Chanelisms": black and white, diamond quilting, the interlocking C logo, the contrasting cap toe, and gilt chains.

Mules
ca. 1994
Bernard Figueroa, American

Bernard Figueroa has been quoted as saying, "There's so much space between a woman's heel and the floor that one can use," and, like Roger Vivier, he took full advantage of it. Figueroa, who designed his own line of couture shoes from 1993 to 2003, is noted for sophisticated designs that pair modern, inventive cuts with quirky sculptured heels. An example is the pair of mules shown here, with its high throat, attractive lavender suede upper, and brown twig-shaped heel. Figueroa was an important figure in the renaissance of the creative interpretation of form that has enlivened shoe design since the early 1990s.

"Munster" Platform Shoes
1994

John Fluevog, Canadian, b. 1948

In 1970, John Fluevog opened his first store with his friend and partner Peter Fox in Vancouver. In 1981, Fox moved to New York and the store closed. Five years later, Fluevog started his own store in Seattle. He soon began designing, and his avant-garde creations—particularly his platform shoes—were a hit with the young.

Shown here in black, Fluevog's "Munster" shoes were made in several styles and colors. A bright orange pair was worn by Lady Miss Kier of Deee-lite on the 1990 cover of *World Clique,* their first album.

Ankle Boots
1994

Byron Lars, American, b. 1965

In 1991, Byron Lars was named "rookie of the year" by *Women's Wear Daily*, and in 2010, he designed the dress that First Lady Michelle Obama wore for a Paul McCartney appearance at the White House. Lars refers to his designs as "twisted American classics," juxtaposing the familiar with the exotic or unusual. To accompany his 1994 Asian-influenced ensemble—which included a red satin baseball jacket with frog closures—Lars blended aspects of a 1970s platform shoe and a *geta,* a Japanese wood clog. His white leather boot with its black leather trompe l'oeil thong strap and wood sole approximates a geta worn with a *tabi,* the traditional Japanese bifurcated-toe sock. Like the geta, the sole has two flat risers, but here, they have migrated to the front part of the shoe.

Opposite page:
In this detail of *Yukihira and Two Brinemaidens at Suma,* an eighteenth-century hanging scroll by Okumura Masanobu (Japanese, 1686–1764), a geisha is taking a stroll with a young man wearing a pair of *geta* with *tabi.*

"On Liberty" Boots
1994–95

Vivienne Westwood, British, b. 1941

V ivienne Westwood's sexy black leather boots with their platform and high stiletto heel hardly seem to go with the red plaid suit (right) they were designed for. But notice the bustle on the skirt. Westwood has been scrupulous in her study of historical forms of dress. However, her brilliance has been not in the rendering of period artifacts but in the application of contemporary techniques to their form-making and a revivification of their sexual content. Despite her cartoonlike rendering of the bustle, the suit precipitated a surprisingly erotic response when worn with the boots and seen in motion on the runway.

Sandals
ca. 1995

Christian Louboutin, French, b. 1964

After training with Charles Jourdan, creating designs for fashion houses such as Chanel and Yves Saint Laurent, and helping to organize a retrospective for Roger Vivier, Christian Louboutin left the fashion industry in 1989 to pursue garden design. By 1992, he was back and had his own label and a boutique in Paris. Louboutin's love of nature, however, has been a continuing source of inspiration for his shoe designs.

In the mid-1990s, he designed platform sandals with hand-dried flower petals from his garden encased in the clear Lucite soles and heels. For the example shown here with black patent-leather uppers, he used rose petals.

Shoes
2001

American

A style widely worn by exotic dancers, this clear plastic shoe from the Pleaser company has a high arch, a platform that lengthens the leg, and an ankle strap that anchors the shoe securely. All the effects of the heel are enhanced by the visual insubstantiality of the shoe. Cinderella's glass slipper—transparent and fragile— has a subtext of innocence. In the Pleaser shoe, the glass slipper has become plastic and mutated into an eroticized high-heel platform, less about transparency and disclosure than about invisibility and sexual subterfuge.

The shoes worn on the runway with spring/summer 2009 fashions by design duo Scherer Gonzales combine the sexy transparency of the Pleaser shoes with colorful floral decorations. The flowers suspended in the clear platform soles are evocative of the petal-strewn Lucite soles of Christian Louboutin's mid-1990s platform sandals.

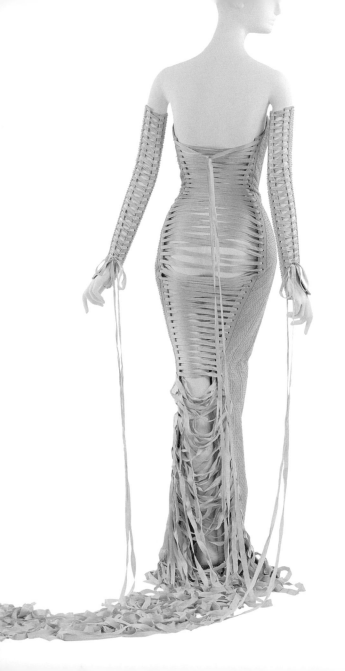

"Des Robes qui se Dérobent"
Evening Shoes
2001

Jean Paul Gaultier, French, b. 1952

Except for the powder-pink color and silk fabric, Jean Paul Gaultier's modestly cut shoes give no clue to the radical look of the evening gown at left for which he designed them. Gaultier is known for his sensational and slightly scandalous runway presentations, and this gown certainly caused a shock as the model wearing it turned around. Playing on the details of nineteenth-century corsetry, the back of the gown consists only of the corset's lacings, which are pulled taut to the knees, where they open into loose loops that form a train of streamers. As Gaultier said, "It is the ultimate 'backless' dress."

"Dot" Boots
2002

Manolo Blahnik, British (b. Spain), b. 1942, and
Damien Hirst, British, b. 1965

In an intersection of contemporary art and fashion, shoe designer Manolo Blahnik worked with artist Damien Hirst on the design for these boots. Using a pattern from Hirst's Spot series of paintings, Blahnik exploited the Pop and Op evocations of the identically sized dots in a reprise of the 1960s go-go boot, but with a high, thin stiletto in place of a flat, functional heel.

"Spots have always been a favorite theme with me," said Blahnik, "but I love the way that Hirst places them in this rigid, repetitive format. It looks very disciplined but at the same time is very playful—thanks to the fun colors that represent chemicals, giving the whole piece a dark undertone, which I find very clever."

An art lover stops to look at *Adrenochrome Semicarbazone Sulfonate* (1992), one of Damien Hirst's early Spot paintings.

Boots
2003

Alexander McQueen, British, 1969–2010

Alexander McQueen (right) has been hailed for challenging perceptions of the role of fashion in political, social, and cultural criticism. His collections were often thematic interpretations alluding to dramatic media events—such as the controversial 1996 "Highland Rape" collection of tattered dresses worn on the runway by "bloodied" models. Credited alongside peers such as John Galliano with the return of artistry to couture in the 1990s, McQueen was awarded a CBE (Commander of the British Empire) in 2003.

These "pirate" boots, with their turned-down cuffs, are from McQueen's spring/summer 2003 "Transitions" collection, which was based on the idea of a shipwreck at sea and consequent landfall in the Amazon.

Sandals
2003

Dolce & Gabbana, Italian, founded 1982

Domenico Dolce (b. 1958) and Stefano Gabbana (b. 1962) are famous for their knowing manipulations of sexual stereotypes, subverting culturally bound expectations even as they embrace and exaggerate familiar attributes of gender. Their men's collections exhibit a flamboyance that is rarely found in business suits, and their women's collections display an overt sex appeal.

At right, model Gisele Bündchen walks down the runway at the showing of Dolce & Gabbana's spring 2003 collection during Milan Fashion Week. The feminine effect created by the silky fabric and trailing drawstrings of the dress and gloves is accompanied by an element of almost discordant historicizing masculinity: calf-high studded black leather gladiator sandals.

Shoe
2004

Yves Saint Laurent, French (b. Algeria), 1936–2008

Yves Saint Laurent's work often followed themes, usually taken from literature, art, or music. He was known for maintaining timely design concepts and hailed for the structured elegance of his creations. Perhaps one of his most defining leitmotifs, however, was a love for the beauty of fur and feathers. From the fur-edged jackets of his "Russian" collection to the wispy embroidered feathers of his famed bird-of-paradise dress (left), Saint Laurent introduced to his designs an atavistic elegance.

This shoe was a prototype for an Yves Saint Laurent Rive Gauche collection that was never actually produced. In Saint Laurent's design, clipped midnight-black feathers were applied to a glamorous black stiletto, conveying the seductive dynamism of the Rive Gauche femme fatale of the runway.

"Bhutan" Shoes
2006

Manolo Blahnik, British (b. Spain), b. 1942

If the television series *Sex and the City* expanded Blahnik's franchise into more populist precincts, it did not change the designer's impulse to push the boundaries of his work. With this "no heel" wedge, a style first explored in his fall/winter 1979–80 collection and repeated in different variations over the years, Blahnik conflates a number of references and locates them in the tradition of the isolated kingdom of Bhutan. For all its vertiginous impracticality, the design is finished with the coarser details of a functional shoe. One imagines that in Blahnik's fictive Bhutan—like Shangri-la, far above the Himalayan cloud line—even peasant women teeter on such shoes like ballerinas or Han dancers.

"This is the kind of work I love to do because it is free from commercial constraints," says Blahnik. "With shoes like these, I don't ever think of selling. They just satisfy the creative craving that I get."

Platform Shoes
2008

Christian Louboutin, French, b. 1964,
for Rodarte, American, founded 2005

As a teenager, Christian Louboutin (right) got a job at the Folies Bergères, where he "learned that shoes are all about posture and proportion." After training with Charles Jourdan, Louboutin freelanced for Chanel, Maud Frizon, and other haute couture houses before opening his first shop in Paris in 1992.

Louboutin says his signature (and trademarked) red soles came about when he was working on a prototype and "realized that the black sole of the shoe was too dark" for his Pop Art–inspired shoes. The solution? He painted the soles with red nail polish borrowed from an assistant.

For the fall/winter 2008 fashion collection from Rodarte, Louboutin created platform stilettos with extremely high heels, buckled straps, studs, and spikes that are evocative of fetish shoes. The example shown here is part of an ensemble that includes a loose-knit dress and tights.

THE CRAFTING OF A HANDMADE SHOE

Today, most shoes are made in factories, but there are still a few shoemakers who produce shoes by hand. These shoemakers have to be skilled artisans in order to maintain the designer's vision while creating a well-made shoe with a beautiful— and comfortable—fit.

The first step in custom shoemaking is creating a last, the form around which each shoe will be molded. A separate last has to be created for each style, in each size, and for each width. Even if two different styles are being made for the same person, new lasts will have to be created for different heel heights and toe shapes.

Lastmakers have to take many different measurements into consideration, among them the length and width of the foot, the height of the big toe, the toe character, the girth of the foot at

A worker touches up the top lift on a high-heel shoe at the Massaro shoemaker workshop in Paris.

various points, the line of the instep from toe to ankle, the angle of the arch, and the way the foot will move inside the shoe. The measurements of the final design sketch are marked off on the last, and a paper pattern of the upper is made. This pattern is also checked against the last and then used to cut out the leather for the upper. A separate, slightly smaller pattern is cut for the lining.

Next, the leather pieces of the upper are sewn together, or closed, leaving a margin around the bottom that will be attached to the insole. A counter is added and, if called for, a toe box. After the insole is attached to the last, the closed leather upper is molded around the last, tacked in place, and left for two weeks to assume the shape of the last.

Once the shoe is ready, the outer sole is cut and attached. Afterward, it is held on a lapstone and pounded into shape with a mallet. The sole is then cemented to the bottom of the upper.

A breasted heel is attached before the sole, as the latter will cover both the bottom of the shoe and the inner side, or breast, of the heel. Any cloth or leather covering is cemented to the heel before the heel is nailed to the shoe. The top lift may be attached to the bottom of the heel before or after the heel has been fastened to the shoe.

After the heel and sole have been attached, the sole is trimmed and the edge is stained, and if made of smooth leather, the outside of the shoe is polished. The shoe is then removed from the last, the sock lining is attached, and the shoe is complete.

GLOSSARY

appliqué: To cut out fabric pieces and sew them to a larger piece of material for decoration; also, the individual cutout fabric pieces

bar tack: A series of back-and-forth stitches used to reinforce a stress point

chopine: A shoe on a raised platform that was popular in Europe from the fifteenth to seventeenth century

counter: A stiffener attached to the inside back of a shoe, added to help strengthen and keep the shape of the quarter

embroidery: Decorative needlework

foot-binding: The process of bending the four smaller toes of a young girl under the foot and folding the forepart of the foot back toward the heel in order to create a small footprint, a custom widely practiced in China from the tenth to the early twentieth century

geta: A Japanese clog with a raised wood sole held on the foot with a thong

golden lotus: In China, a bound foot that was no longer than three inches

heel: A piece added to the bottom rear of the sole to raise the back of the shoe higher than the vamp

heel breast: The front-facing inner surface of the heel

insole: The layer of material between the sock lining and the sole

last: The form, traditionally made out of hardwood, around which a shoe is molded; today, lasts are often made out of high-density plastic

latchet shoe: A shoe with extended shanks that pass over the instep and are fastened with a buckle or a lace

lotus shoe: A small Chinese shoe that was made to fit a bound foot

moccasin: Traditionally, a Native American shoe constructed with a single piece of soft leather brought up around the foot and joined with seams at front and back; also, a modern shoe shaped to look like a moccasin

mule: A backless shoe

open toe: An opening in the front of a shoe

outer sole: The outer bottom part of the sole; also called an outsole

oxford: A closed lace-up shoe

peep-toe: A tiny opening in the front of an otherwise closed-toe shoe

platform: A shoe with a thick bottom unit to add height

pointe shoe: A ballet shoe with a hard reinforced toe

pump: A woman's dress shoe with a closed back and, usually, closed sides and a medium to high heel

quarter: The back quarter of the upper; quarters are usually joined with a seam at the back

sandal: An open shoe that is fastened to the foot by straps

shank: The side of the upper between the vamp and the quarter; also, the steel component between the sole and the insole that gives support to the arch of the foot

slipper: A light, low-cut shoe that can be easily slipped on and off the foot; also, a shoe meant to be worn indoors

sock lining: The piece of material that covers the insole

sole: See *insole* and *outer sole*

stiletto: A very high, narrow heel; the word *stiletto* means "dagger" in Italian

***tabi*:** Traditional Japanese ankle socks with a separation between the big toe and the other toes

thong: A thin piece of material that separates the big toe from the other toes; also a shoe, usually a sandal, that has a thong

throat: The topline of the vamp where it meets the instep

toe box: A stiffener inside the toe of a shoe

toe character: The angle of the front of the foot from the little toe to the big toe

tongue: The part of shoe behind the laces; also, a raised piece that extends above the regular throat line

top lift: The small bottom section of a heel

topline: The top edge of the upper

turn-shoe: A shoe with the upper and sole sewed together while it is inside out; when finished, the shoe is turned right-side out so that the seams are on the inside

upper: The part of the shoe above the sole

vamp: The front part of the upper covering the toes and part of the instep

PARTS OF A SHOE

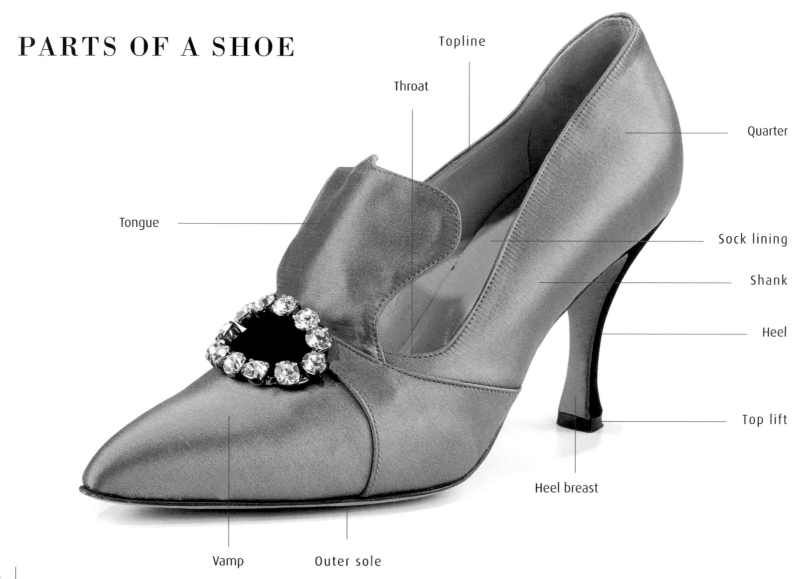

Topline

Throat

Quarter

Tongue

Sock lining

Shank

Heel

Top lift

Heel breast

Vamp

Outer sole

CREDITS

The works of art in this book are from the collection of The Metropolitan Museum of Art, unless otherwise noted. Every reasonable effort has been made to identify and contact copyright holders but in some cases, they could not be traced. If you hold or administer rights for works of art published here, please contact us. Any errors or omissions will be corrected in subsequent printings.

FRONT COVER:
"Portrait" Shoes
Vivienne Westwood, British, b. 1941
Leather, 1990
Millia Davenport and Zipporah Fleisher Fund, 2006   2006.14a, b

BACK COVER:
Evening boot designed by Roger Vivier
Photograph: Paul Schutzer/Time & Life Pictures/Getty Images

TITLE PAGE AND PAGE 4:
Evening Shoes
Roger Vivier, French, 1913–1998, for House of Dior, French, founded 1947
Silk, rhinestones, beads, 1954
Gift of Valerian Stux-Rybar, 1980   1980.597.14

PAGE 5:
Sarah Jessica Parker, May 2010
Photograph: Kevin Mazur/WireImage

PAGE 6:
Shoes
French, 1690–1700
Silk, leather
Rogers Fund, 1906   06.1344a, b

Court Presentation Shoes
American or European, 1896
Silk
Brooklyn Museum Costume Collection at The Metropolitan Museum of Art, Gift of the Brooklyn Museum, 2009; Anonymous gift, in memory of Mrs. John Roebling, 1970   2009.300.941d, e

PAGE 7:
Shoes
Christian Louboutin, French, b. 1963, for Rodarte, American, founded 2005
Leather, metal, fall/winter 2008–09
Purchase, Gilles Bensimon Inc. Gift, 2009   2009.422d, e

PAGE 8:
Chopines
Probably Italian, 1550–1650
Silk, metal
Brooklyn Museum Costume Collection at The Metropolitan Museum of Art, Gift of the Brooklyn Museum, 2009; Gift of Herman Delman, 1955
2009.300.1494a, b

PAGE 9:
Venetian Courtesan
French School, 16th century
Colored engraving
BIBLIOTHÈQUE NATIONAL, Paris
Photograph: Giraudon/The Bridgeman Art Library International

PAGE 10:
The Family of the Grand Dauphin (detail)
Pierre Mignard, French, 1612–1695
Oil on canvas, 91½ x 119⅔ in., 1687
CHATEAUX DE VERSAILLES ET DE TRIANON, Versailles
Photograph: Réunion des Musées Nationaux/Art Resource, New York

PAGE 11:
Shoes
French, 1690–1700
Silk, leather
Rogers Fund, 1906   06.1344a, b

PAGE 12:
Latchet Shoes
British, 1750–69
Wool, linen, silk
Brooklyn Museum Costume Collection at The Metropolitan Museum of Art, Gift of the Brooklyn Museum, 2009; Gift of Mrs. Clarence R. Hyde, 1928   2009.300.1407a, b

PAGE 13:
Latchet Shoes
British, 1700–29
Wool, linen, metal
Brooklyn Museum Costume Collection at The Metropolitan Museum of Art, Gift of the Brooklyn Museum, 2009; Gift of Mrs. Clarence R. Hyde, 1928   2009.300.1411a, b

PAGE 14:
Slippers
Probably British, 1790–1805
Leather
Brooklyn Museum Costume Collection at The Metropolitan Museum of Art, Gift of the Brooklyn Museum, 2009; Gift of Herman Delman, 1954
2009.300.1484a, b

PAGE 15:
Young Woman Drawing (detail)
Marie-Denise Villers, French, 1774–1821
Oil on canvas, 63½ x 50⅝ in., 1801
Mr. and Mrs. Isaac D. Fletcher Collection, Bequest of Isaac D. Fletcher, 1917   17.120.204

PAGE 16:
Lotus Shoes
Chinese, 1800–1943
Silk, cotton
Gift of Mrs. Robert Woods Bliss, 1943   C.I.43.90.60a, b

PAGE 17:
Lily Foot Model
Chinese (Han peoples), 19th century
Plaster
The Jacqueline Loewe Fowler Costume Collection, Gift of Jacqueline Loewe Fowler, 1982   1982.82.16a

PAGE 18:
Pedestal Shoes
Chinese (Manchu peoples), 19th century
Silk, leather, cotton, wood
Gift of Mrs. Van S. Merle-Smith, 1941   C.I.41.110.272a, b

PAGE 19:
The Empress of China Cixi (Tsu-Hsi), 1903
Photograph: Three Lions/Getty Images

PAGES 20–21:
Slippers
British, ca. 1825
Silk
Brooklyn Museum Costume Collection at The Metropolitan Museum of Art, Gift of the Brooklyn Museum, 2009; Designated Purchase Fund, 1981
2009.300.1611a, b

PAGE 21:
Moccasins
American, 19th century
Leather, porcupine quills, beads
PEABODY ESSEX MUSEUM, Salem, Massachusetts
Photograph: © Peaboy Essex Museum/The Bridgeman Art Library International

PAGES 22–23:
Ankle Boots and Pattens
American, 1825–30
Leather
Brooklyn Museum Costume Collection at The Metropolitan Museum of
Art, Gift of the Brooklyn Museum, 2009; Gift of Herman Delman, 1954
2009.300.1488a–f

PAGE 24:
Maria Taglioni (1804–1884) in La Sylphide, Souvenir d'Adieu
Marie Alexandre Alophe, French, 1812–1883
Color lithograph, ca. 1832
BIBLIOTHÈQUE DES ARTS DECORATIFS, Paris
Photograph: Archives Charmet/The Bridgeman Art Library International

PAGES 24–25:
Evening Slippers
Probably American, 1835–45
Silk
Brooklyn Museum Costume Collection at The Metropolitan Museum of
Art, Gift of the Brooklyn Museum, 2009; Gift of Herman Delman, 1954
2009.300.1460a, b

PAGE 26:
Young Misses' and Children's Fashions for October (detail)
The Peterson Magazine, 1864, print
Picture Collection, The New York Public Library, Astor, Lenox, and Tilden
Foundations

PAGE 27:
Evening Boots
French, 1860–69
Silk
Brooklyn Museum Costume Collection at The Metropolitan Museum of
Art, Gift of the Brooklyn Museum, 2009; Gift of Mrs. G. Brinton Roberts,
1946 2009.300.1439a–d

PAGE 28:
Portrait of Jeanne Duval (detail)
Édouard Manet, French, 1832–1883
Oil on canvas, 44⁷⁄₁₆ x 35⅜ in., 1862
MUSEUM OF FINE ARTS (SZEPMUVESZETI MUZEUM), Budapest
Photograph: Giraudon/Art Resource, New York

PAGE 29:
Slippers
Julien Mayer, French
Cotton, silk, ca. 1870
Brooklyn Museum Costume Collection at The Metropolitan Museum of
Art, Gift of the Brooklyn Museum, 2009; Gift of Herman Delman, 1954
2009.300.1465a, b

PAGE 30:
Carriage Boots
American, 1870–90
Wool, fur, leather
Brooklyn Museum Costume Collection at The Metropolitan Museum of
Art, Gift of the Brooklyn Museum, 2009; Gift of Mrs. Jason Westerfield,
1967 2009.300.1586a–d

PAGE 31:
Central Park in Winter (detail)
Currier & Ives, American, active 1857–1907
Hand-colored lithograph, 13⅜ x 17⁹⁄₁₆ in., 1877–94
Bequest of Adele S. Colgate, 1962 63.550.337

PAGE 32:
Pumps
French, 1873
Silk, metal
Gift of Mrs. Stewart Waller, 1950 C.I.50.12.1a, b

PAGE 33:
Pumps
Hellstern and Sons, French
Silk, 1870s
Purchase, Irene Lewisohn Bequest, 1973 1973.260.4a, b

PAGE 34:
Evening Shoes
French, 1875–85
Silk, glass
Brooklyn Museum Costume Collection at The Metropolitan Museum
of Art, Gift of the Brooklyn Museum, 2009; Gift of Mrs. Frederick H.
Prince Jr., 1967 2009.300.1582a, b

PAGE 35:
Evening Shoes
French, 1875–85
Silk
Brooklyn Museum Costume Collection at The Metropolitan Museum
of Art, Gift of the Brooklyn Museum, 2009; Gift of Mrs. Frederick H.
Prince Jr., 1967 2009.300.1581a, b

PAGES 36–37:
Evening Slippers
J. Ferry, French
Silk, 1880
Brooklyn Museum Costume Collection at The Metropolitan Museum
of Art, Gift of the Brooklyn Museum, 2009; Gift of Mrs. Frederick H.
Prince Jr., 1967 2009.300.1584a, b

PAGES 38–39:
Evening Boots
Probably French, 1885–90
Silk, metal
Brooklyn Museum Costume Collection at The Metropolitan Museum of
Art, Gift of the Brooklyn Museum, 2009; Gift of Herman Delman, 1954
2009.300.1477a–d

PAGES 40–41:
Evening Shoes
A. J. Cammeyer, American, department store
Leather, 1889–93
Brooklyn Museum Costume Collection at The Metropolitan Museum of
Art, Gift of the Brooklyn Museum, 2009; Gift of Marion Fisher, 1952
2009.300.1455a–d

PAGES 42–43:
Juliet Slippers
Rosenbloom's, American, department store
Leather, ca. 1892
Brooklyn Museum Costume Collection at The Metropolitan Museum of
Art, Gift of the Brooklyn Museum, 2009; Gift of Charllne Osgood, 1965
2009.300.1555a, b

PAGE 44:
Court Presentation Shoes
American or European, 1896
Silk
Brooklyn Museum Costume Collection at The Metropolitan Museum of
Art, Gift of the Brooklyn Museum, 2009; Anonymous gift, in memory of
Mrs. John Roebling, 1970 2009.300.941d, e

PAGE 45:
Portrait of Emily Warren Roebling (detail)
Charles-Émile-Auguste Carolus-Duran, French, 1838–1917
Oil on canvas, 89 x 47½ in., 1896
THE BROOKLYN MUSEUM, Brooklyn
Gift of Paul Roebling, 1994 1994.69.1

PAGE 46:
Pumps
J. Ferry, French
Leather, silk, ca. 1906
Brooklyn Museum Costume Collection at The Metropolitan Museum
of Art, Gift of the Brooklyn Museum, 2009; Gift of Mrs. Frederick H.
Prince Jr., 1967 2009.300.1580a, b

PAGE 47:
Pumps
American, 1900
Leather, metal
Brooklyn Museum Costume Collection at The Metropolitan Museum of
Art, Gift of the Brooklyn Museum, 2009; Brooklyn Museum Collection
2009.300.1638a, b

PAGES 48–49:
Pumps
Pietro Yantorny, Italian, 1874–1936
Silk, rhinestones, 1913–18
Gift of Elizabeth Hudson, 1969 C.I.69.12.2a, b

PAGE 50:
Evening Shoes
Pietro Yantorny, Italian, 1874–1936
Silk, metal, jet, 1914–19
Brooklyn Museum Costume Collection at The Metropolitan Museum of
Art, Gift of the Brooklyn Museum, 2009; Gift of Mercedes de Acosta,
1953 2009.300.1178a, b

PAGE 51:
Cyclamen—Mrs. Philip Lydig (detail)
Edward Steichen, American (b. Luxembourg), 1879–1973
Direct carbon print, 12⅜ x 8½ in., ca. 1905
Alfred Stieglitz Collection, 1933 33.43.9

Shoes
Pietro Yantorny, Italian, 1874–1936
Silk, metal, glass, 1914–19
Gift of Capezio Inc., 1953 C.I.53.76.10–21a, b

PAGE 52:
Mules
Pietro Yantorny, Italian, 1874–1936
Silk, metal, 1914–19
Brooklyn Museum Costume Collection at The Metropolitan Museum of
Art, Gift of the Brooklyn Museum, 2009; Gift of Mercedes de Acosta,
1953 2009.300.1459a, b

PAGE 53:
Women of Algiers in Their Apartment (detail)
Eugène Delacroix, French, 1798–1863
Oil on canvas, 70⅞ x 90³⁄₁₆ in., 1834
MUSÉE DU LOUVRE, Paris
Photograph: Erich Lessing/Art Resource, New York

PAGE 54:
Evening Boots
Bray Bros., American, department store
Leather, ca. 1918
Brooklyn Museum Costume Collection at The Metropolitan Museum of
Art, Gift of the Brooklyn Museum, 2009; Gift of Mrs. Roderick Tower,
1961 2009.300.1536a–d

PAGE 55:
Café Riche Tango Show
Georges Redon, French, 1869–1943
Poster, ca. 1914
Photograph: Apic/Getty Images

PAGE 56:
Shoes
Charles Strohbeck Inc., American, manufacturer
Leather, ca. 1920
Brooklyn Museum Costume Collection at The Metropolitan Museum of
Art, Gift of the Brooklyn Museum, 2009; Gift of Charles Strohbeck, 1964
2009.300.1551a, b

PAGE 57:
Evening Shoes
Charles Strohbeck Inc., American, manufacturer
Cotton, silk, ca. 1920
Brooklyn Museum Costume Collection at The Metropolitan Museum of
Art, Gift of the Brooklyn Museum, 2009; Gift of Charles Strohbeck, 1964
2009.300.3265a, b

PAGES 58–59:
"Le Bal" Slippers
André Perugia, French, 1893–1977, for Paul Poiret, French, 1879–1944
Silk, glass, leather, 1924
Purchase, Friends of The Costume Institute Gifts, 2005 2005.192a, b

PAGES 60–61:
Shoes
Pietro Yantorny, Italian, 1874–1936
Leather, 1925–30
Brooklyn Museum Costume Collection at The Metropolitan Museum of
Art, Gift of the Brooklyn Museum, 2009; Gift of Mrs. Edward G. Sparrow,
1969 2009.300.2144a–d

PAGE 62:
Juliette Compton, ca. 1920s
Photograph © John Spring Collection/Corbis

PAGE 63:
Evening Shoes
Marshall Field & Co., American, founded 1881, department store
Leather, rhinestones, ca. 1927
Brooklyn Museum Costume Collection at The Metropolitan Museum of
Art, Gift of the Brooklyn Museum, 2009; Gift of Herman Delman, 1955
2009.300.1206a, b

PAGES 64–65:
Oxfords
Thomas, British, department store
Leather, ca. 1927
Brooklyn Museum Costume Collection at The Metropolitan Museum of
Art, Gift of the Brooklyn Museum, 2009; Gift of Rodman A. Heeren, 1960
2009.300.3783a–d

PAGES 66–67:
Evening Sandals
André Perugia, French, 1893–1977
Leather, metal, 1928–29
Brooklyn Museum Costume Collection at The Metropolitan Museum of
Art, Gift of the Brooklyn Museum, 2009; Gift of Mrs. Carleton Putnam,
1981 2009.300.1612a, b

PAGES 68–69:
Evening Shoes
Delman, American, founded 1919, manufacturer
Silk, leather, synthetic, rhinestones, 1935–40
Brooklyn Museum Costume Collection at The Metropolitan Museum of
Art, Gift of the Brooklyn Museum, 2009; Gift of Herman Delman, 1955
2009.300.1207a, b

PAGES 70–71:
Pumps
French, 1935–49
Leather
Brooklyn Museum Costume Collection at The Metropolitan Museum of
Art, Gift of the Brooklyn Museum, 2009; Gift of Rodman A. Heeren, 1962
2009.300.1295a, b

PAGE 72:
Platform Sandals
Salvatore Ferragamo, Italian, 1898–1960
Leather, silk, metal, rhinestones, 1938
Brooklyn Museum Costume Collection at The Metropolitan Museum of
Art, Gift of the Brooklyn Museum, 2009; Gift of Brooklyn Museum Fair,
1956 2009.300.1505a, b

PAGE 73:
Platform Sandal
Salvatore Ferragamo, Italian, 1898–1960
Leather, cork, 1938
Gift of Salvatore Ferragamo, 1973   1973.282.2

PAGE 74:
Salvatore Ferragamo in his Florence workshop, 1956
Photograph: Keystone/Getty Images

PAGE 75:
Shoe
Salvatore Ferragamo, Italian, 1898–1960
Leather, 1948–50
Gift of Salvatore Ferragamo, 1973   1973.282.6

PAGE 76:
Ankle Boots
André Perugia, French, 1893–1977
Leather, ca. 1939
Brooklyn Museum Costume Collection at The Metropolitan Museum
of Art, Gift of the Brooklyn Museum, 2009; Gift of Millicent Huttleston
Rogers, 1951   2009.300.3136a, b

PAGE 77:
André Perugia in a shoe factory, 1951
Photograph © Bettmann/Corbis

PAGE 78:
Pumps
Attributed to André Perugia, French, 1893–1977, for Elsa Schiaparelli,
Italian, 1890–1973
Silk, 1939
Brooklyn Museum Costume Collection at The Metropolitan Museu n
of Art, Gift of the Brooklyn Museum, 2009; Gift of Arturo and
Paul Peralta-Ramos, 1954   2009.300.3519a, b

PAGE 79:
Shoe Hat
Elsa Schiaparelli, Italian, 1890–1973
Wool, fall/winter 1937–38
Gift of Rose Messing, 1974   1974.139

PAGES 80–81:
Evening Shoes
Steven Arpad, French (b. Hungary), 1904–1999, for House of Balenciaga,
French, founded 1937
Silk, wood, 1939
Brooklyn Museum Costume Collection at The Metropolitan Museum
of Art, Gift of the Brooklyn Museum, 2009; Gift of Arpad, 1947
2009.300.1394a, b

PAGE 82:
Shoe (Prototype), Model No. 152
Steven Arpad, French (b. Hungary), 1904–1999
Leather, wood, 1939
Brooklyn Museum Costume Collection at The Metropolitan Museum
of Art, Gift of the Brooklyn Museum, 2009; Gift of Arpad, 1947
2009.300.1130

Shoe (Prototype), Model No. 266
Steven Arpad, French (b. Hungary), 1904–1999
Leather, wood, 1939
Brooklyn Museum Costume Collection at The Metropolitan Museum
of Art, Gift of the Brooklyn Museum, 2009; Gift of Arpad, 1947
2009.300.1143

PAGE 83:
Shoe (Prototype), Model No. 463
Steven Arpad, French (b. Hungary), 1904–1999
Silk, leather, wood, 1939
Brooklyn Museum Costume Collection at The Metropolitan Museum
of Art, Gift of the Brooklyn Museum, 2009; Gift of Arpad, 1947
2009.300.1145

PAGES 84–85:
Ankle Boots
Steven Arpad, French (b. Hungary), 1904–1999, for House of Balenciaga,
French, founded 1937
Leather, 1939
Brooklyn Museum Costume Collection at The Metropolitan Museum
of Art, Gift of the Brooklyn Museum, 2009; Gift of Arpad, 1947
2009.300.1392a, b

PAGES 86–87:
Evening Shoes
Steven Arpad, French (b. Hungary), 1904–1999; Delman, American,
founded 1919, manufacturer
Leather, 1939
Brooklyn Museum Costume Collection at The Metropolitan Museum of
Art, Gift of the Brooklyn Museum, 2009; Gift of Herbert Delman, 1955
2009.300.1205a, b

PAGES 88–89:
Platform Sandals
Victor, American
Leather, ca. 1940
Brooklyn Museum Costume Collection at The Metropolitan Museum of
Art, Gift of the Brooklyn Museum, 2009; Gift of Vivian Mook Baer in
memory of Sylvia Terner Mook, 1983   2009.300.1614a, b

PAGE 90:
Platform Sandals
Penét Shoes Inc., American, manufacturer
Leather, ca. 1943
Brooklyn Museum Costume Collection at The Metropolitan Museum of
Art, Gift of the Brooklyn Museum, 2009; Gift of Mrs. Lewis Iselin Jr., 1960
2009.300.1530a, b

PAGE 91:
Carmen Miranda displaying her platform shoes, 1944
Photograph © Bettmann/Corbis

PAGE 92:
"Invisible" Sandals
Salvatore Ferragamo, Italian, 1898–1960
Leather, synthetic, 1947
Brooklyn Museum Costume Collection at The Metropolitan Museum of
Art, Gift of the Brooklyn Museum, 2009; Gift of Mrs. R. L. Gilpatric, 1960
2009.300.3781a, b

PAGE 93:
"Luito" Shoes
Salvatore Ferragamo, Italian, 1898–1960
Leather, synthetic, 1947–50
Brooklyn Museum Costume Collection at The Metropolitan Museum of
Art, Gift of the Brooklyn Museum, 2009; Gift of Brooklyn Museum Fair,
1956   2009.300.1244a, b

PAGE 94:
Flag
Jasper Johns, American, b. 1930
Encaustic, oil, and collage on fabric mounted on plywood, three panels,
42¼ x 60⅝ in., 1954–55
THE MUSEUM OF MODERN ART, New York
Gift of Philip Johnson in honor of Alfred H. Barr, Jr.
Art © Jasper Johns/Licensed by VAGA, New York, NY
Photograph: Digital Image © The Museum of Modern Art/Licensed by
SCALA/Art Resource, New York

PAGE 95:
Platform Sandals
Dominick LaValle, American
Leather, metal, ca. 1950
Gift of Carroll F. Cook, in memory of his grandparents,
Mr. and Mrs. Dominick LaValle, 1987   1987.303.1b, c

PAGE 96:
Marabou Mules
American, 1950–59
Synthetic, feathers
Brooklyn Museum Costume Collection at The Metropolitan Museum of
Art, Gift of the Brooklyn Museum, 2009; Gift of Joan Fontaine, 1962
2009.300.1537a, b

PAGE 97:
Marilyn Monroe in a scene from The Seven Year Itch, 1957
Photograph: AFP/Getty Images

PAGE 98:
Tony and Sally DeMarco performing, 1941
Photograph: Gjon Mili/Time & Life Pictures/Getty Images

PAGE 99:
Dance Shoes
Palter DeLiso Inc., American, 1927–75, manufacturer
Leather, silk, rhinestones, 1951
Brooklyn Museum Costume Collection at The Metropolitan Museum of Art, Gift of the Brooklyn Museum, 2009; Gift of Mr. and Mrs. Tony DeMarco, 1962   2009.300.3830a, b

PAGE 100:
Shoes
Hubert de Givenchy, French, b. 1927; André Perugia, French, 1893–1977
Straw, 1952
Brooklyn Museum Costume Collection at The Metropolitan Museum of Art, Gift of the Brooklyn Museum, 2009; Gift of Mrs. Lewis Iselin Jr., 1960
2009.300.3785a, b

PAGE 101:
Hubert de Givenchy, Cobina Wright, and Sara Shane at the premiere of So Big, 1953
Photograph: Archive Photos/Getty Images

PAGES 102–03:
Stocking Shoes
Beth Levine, American, 1914–2006
Silk, synthetic, 1953
Brooklyn Museum Costume Collection at The Metropolitan Museum of Art, Gift of the Brooklyn Museum, 2009; Gift of Beth Levine in memory of her husband, Herbert, 1994   2009.300.2240a, b

PAGE 103:
Model wearing Levine stocking shoes
Photograph: Gjon Mili/Time & Life Pictures/Getty Images

PAGES 104–05:
Sandal
Italian, 1954–58
Leather
Brooklyn Museum Costume Collection at The Metropolitan Museum of Art, Gift of the Brooklyn Museum, 2009; Gift of Charline Osgood, 1960
2009.300.1274

PAGE 106:
Shoes
European, 1690–1710
Leather, silk
Brooklyn Museum Costume Collection at The Metropolitan Museum of Art, Gift of the Brooklyn Museum, 2009; Gift of Herman Delman, 1954
2009.300.1478a, b

PAGE 107:
Shoe
Enzo Albanese, Italian, 1933–2003
Leather, 1954–58
Brooklyn Museum Costume Collection at The Metropolitan Museum of Art, Gift of the Brooklyn Museum, 2009; Gift of Charline Osgood, 1960
2009.300.1531

PAGES 108–09:
Sandals
Mario Valentino, Italian, 1927–1991
Leather, 1955
Brooklyn Museum Costume Collection at The Metropolitan Museum of Art, Gift of the Brooklyn Museum, 2009; Gift of Charline Osgood, 1960
2009.300.1270a, b

PAGE 110:
Topless Shoes
Beth Levine, American, 1914–2006
Leather, synthetic, 1955–60
Brooklyn Museum Costume Collection at The Metropolitan Museum of Art, Gift of the Brooklyn Museum, 2009; Gift of Beth Levine
2009.300.3918a, b

PAGE 111:
Topless Shoes
Beth Levine, American, 1914–2006
Leather, 1955–60
Brooklyn Museum Costume Collection at The Metropolitan Museum of Art, Gift of the Brooklyn Museum, 2009; Gift of Beth Levine
2009.300.3917a, b

PAGE 112:
Beth Levine, Golden Beach, Florida, 1999
Photograph © Bruce Weber

PAGE 113:
Sandals
Beth Levine, American, 1914–2006
Synthetic, ca. 1968
Gift of The Fashion Group Inc., 1975   1975.295.12a, b

PAGES 114–15:
Sandal
Enzo Albanese, Italian, 1933–2003
Leather, metal, ca. 1958
Brooklyn Museum Costume Collection at The Metropolitan Museum of Art, Gift of the Brooklyn Museum, 2009; Gift of Margaret Jerrold Inc., 1965   2009.300.1553

PAGE 116:
Cocktail Shoes
David Evins, American (b. England), 1909–1992
Leather, metal, ca. 1958
Brooklyn Museum Costume Collection at The Metropolitan Museum of Art, Gift of the Brooklyn Museum, 2009; Gift of Mrs. Emmet Whitlock, 1985   2009.300.3376a, b

PAGE 117:
The Wedding of Grace Kelly and Prince Rainier of Monaco, April 19, 1956
Photograph: STF/AFP/Getty Images

PAGES 118–19:
Sandals
Domenico Albion, Italian
Leather, 1958
Brooklyn Museum Costume Collection at The Metropolitan Museum of Art, Gift of the Brooklyn Museum, 2009; Gift of Charline Osgood, 1960
2009.300.3793a, b

PAGE 120:
Sandal
Alberto Dal Co', Italian, 1902–1963
Leather, 1958
Brooklyn Museum Costume Collection at The Metropolitan Museum of Art, Gift of the Brooklyn Museum, 2009; Gift of Charline Osgood, 1960
2009.300.3209

PAGE 121:
Picking Persimmons (detail)
Kitagawa Utamaro, Japanese, 1753/54–1806
Triptych of polychrome woodblock prints; ink and color on paper, 15 x 30 in., ca. 1803–04
Gift of Estate of Samuel Isham, 1914   JP994

PAGES 122–23:
Cocktail Shoes
Alberto Dal Co', Italian, 1902–1963
Leather, 1958
Brooklyn Museum Costume Collection at The Metropolitan Museum of Art, Gift of the Brooklyn Museum, 2009; Gift of Charline Osgood, 1960
2009.300.1261a, b

PAGES 124–25:
Shoe
Alberto Dal Co', Italian, 1902–1963
Leather, glass, metal, 1958
Brooklyn Museum Costume Collection at The Metropolitan Museum of Art, Gift of the Brooklyn Museum, 2009; Gift of Charline Osgood, 1960
2009.300.1265

PAGE 126:
A model presents a design by Alexander McQueen, 2007
Photograph: François Guillot/AFP/Getty Images

PAGE 127:
Evening Shoe
Beth Levine, American, 1914–2006
Feathers, leather, 1958
Gift of Beth and Herbert Levine, 1977   1977.287.13

PAGES 128–29:
Boots
Beth Levine, American, 1914–2006
Hair calf, leather, 1959
Gift of Beth and Herbert Levine, 1977   1977.287.23a, b

PAGE 130:
Pump
Mabel Julianelli, American, 1909–1994
Metal, synthetic, late 1950s–early 1960s
Gift of Mabel Julianelli, 1973   1973.237.1

PAGE 131:
"Naked" evening sandal by Mabel Julianelli
Photograph: Nina Leen/Time & Life Pictures/Getty Images

PAGES 132–33:
Evening Shoes
Raphael, Italian, manufacturer
Silk, ca. 1960
Brooklyn Museum Costume Collection at The Metropolitan Museum of
Art, Gift of the Brooklyn Museum, 2009; Brooklyn Museum Collection
2009.300.1639a, b

PAGE 134:
Evening Shoes
Roger Vivier, French, 1913–1998, for House of Dior, French, founded 1947
Silk, 1960
Gift of Valerian Stux-Rybar, 1979   1979.472.24a, b

PAGE 135:
Evening Shoe
Roger Vivier, French, 1913–1998, for House of Dior, French, founded 1947
Silk, feathers, 1960
Gift of Valerian Stux-Rybar, 1980   1980.597.31

PAGES 136–37:
Evening Shoes
Roger Vivier, French, 1913–1998, for House of Dior, French, founded 1947
Silk, metal, leather, synthetic, glass, 1961
Gift of Valerian Stux-Rybar, 1980   1980.597.4a, b

PAGE 138:
Evening Boot
Roger Vivier, French, 1913–1998, for House of Dior, French, founded 1947
Silk, leather, cotton, synthetic, glass, 1957
Gift of Valerian Stux-Rybar, 1980   1980.597.25

PAGE 139:
Roger Vivier, 1996
Photograph: Bardo Fabiani/WireImage

PAGE 140:
Mule
Beth Levine, American, 1914–2006
Leather, silk, 1962
Gift of Beth and Herbert Levine, 1977   1977.287.20

PAGE 141:
Slingback Shoe
Beth Levine, American, 1914–2006
Leather, ca. 1962
Brooklyn Museum Costume Collection at The Metropolitan Museum of
Art, Gift of the Brooklyn Museum, 2009; Gift of Beth Levine in memory
of her husband, Herbert, 1994   2009.300.3907

PAGE 142:
Evening Boots
Beth Levine, American, 1914–2006
Silk, metal, rhinestones, ca. 1962
Brooklyn Museum Costume Collection at The Metropolitan Museum
of Art, Gift of the Brooklyn Museum, 2009; Gift of Lady Emilia Dreher
Armstrong, 1989   2009.300.2230a, b

PAGE 143:
Nancy Sinatra wearing Beth Levine boots, 1960
Photograph: GAB Archive/Redferns

PAGE 144:
Models wearing designs by Emilio Pucci, 1964
Photograph: David Lees/Time & Life Pictures/Getty Images

PAGE 145:
Slippers
Emilio Pucci, Italian, 1914–1992
Leather, fall/winter 1964–65
Gift of Mr. Max Hess, 1965   C.I.65.9.3a, b

PAGES 146–47:
"Kick Off" Shoes
Beth Levine, American, 1914–2006
Leather, ca. 1965
Brooklyn Museum Costume Collection at The Metropolitan Museum of
Art, Gift of the Brooklyn Museum, 2009; Gift of Beth Levine in memory
of her husband, Herbert, 1994   2009.300.3906a, b

PAGE 148:
"Kabuki" Evening Shoe
Beth Levine, American, 1914–2006
Silk, metal, wood, ca. 1965
Brooklyn Museum Costume Collection at The Metropolitan Museum of
Art, Gift of the Brooklyn Museum, 2009; Gift of Beth Levine in memory
of her husband, Herbert, 1994   2009.300.1636

PAGE 149:
"Kabuki" Evening Shoes
Beth Levine, American, 1914–2006
Silk, rhinestones, wood, 1962
Gift of Herbert Levine Inc., 1973   1973.276.25a, b

PAGES 150–51:
Slingback Shoes
Charles Jourdan, French, 1883–1976
Leather, 1965
Brooklyn Museum Costume Collection at The Metropolitan Museum
of Art, Gift of the Brooklyn Museum, 2009; Gift of Jane Holzer, 1986
2009.300.1617a, b

PAGES 152–53:
Racing Car Shoes
Katharina Denzinger, American; Herbert Levine Inc., American, founded
1949, manufacturer
Leather, synthetic, glass, metal, 1965–67
Gift of Herbert Levine Inc., 1973   1973.276.29a, b

PAGES 154–55:
Accessory Set
Shoes by David Evins, American (b. England), 1909–1991
Handbag by Lucille de Paris
Leather, metal, 1965–75
Brooklyn Museum Costume Collection at The Metropolitan Museum of
Art, Gift of the Brooklyn Museum, 2009; Gift of Mrs. Louis Nathanson,
1983   2009.300.2916a–d

PAGE 156:
André Courrèges surrounded by his models, 1968
Photograph © Jack Burlot/Apis/Sygma/Corbis

PAGE 157:
Boots
André Courrèges, French, b. 1923
Leather, ca. 1967
Brooklyn Museum Costume Collection at The Metropolitan Museum of
Art, Gift of the Brooklyn Museum, 2009; Gift of Barbara Hodes, 1985
2009.300.3380a, b

PAGE 158:
Ankle Boots
Pierre Cardin, French, b. 1922
Leather, metal, 1967
Gift of Pierre Cardin, 1977   1977.25.16d, e

PAGE 159:
45-rpm vinyl record
Photograph: Apic/Getty Images

PAGE 160:
Diana Vreeland wearing Roger Vivier boots
Photograph © Copyright by Jonathan Becker, All Rights Reserved

PAGE 161:
Boots
Roger Vivier, French, 1913–1998
Synthetic, leather, late 1960s
Gift of Estate of Diana Vreeland, 1990   1990.64.1a, b

PAGE 162:
Platform Shoes
Dasaje do Brasil, Brazilian, manufacturer
Synthetic, ca. 1973
Brooklyn Museum Costume Collection at The Metropolitan Museum of
Art, Gift of the Brooklyn Museum, 2009; Gift of Mark Isaacson, 1992
2009.300.1629a, b

PAGE 163:
Platform Shoes
Mary Poppins, American, manufacturer
Leather, ca. 1973
Brooklyn Museum Costume Collection at The Metropolitan Museum
of Art, Gift of the Brooklyn Museum, 2009; Gift of Sheri Sandler, 1993
2009.300.3392a, b

PAGE 164:
Pumps
Vivienne Westwood, British, b. 1941
Leather, ca. 1974
Gift of the Estate of Luciana Martinez de la Rosa, 1997   1997.59.1a, b

PAGE 165:
Malcolm McLaren and Vivienne Westwood, 1981
Photograph: Rex USA

PAGES 166–67:
Boots
Kaufmann's, American, department store
Leather, cotton, ca. 1975
Brooklyn Museum Costume Collection at The Metropolitan Museum of
Art, Gift of the Brooklyn Museum, 2009; Gift of Mrs. Mortimer J. Solomon,
1978   2009.300.1610a, b

PAGES 168–69:
Evening Sandals
Hubert de Givenchy, French, b. 1927
Leather, metal, 1980
Brooklyn Museum Costume Collection at The Metropolitan Museum of
Art, Gift of the Brooklyn Museum, 2009; Gift of Mrs. Emmet Whitlock,
1985   2009.300.3375a, b

PAGES 170–71:
Boots
Maud Frizon, French, b. 1941
Leather, 1980s
Gift of Muriel Kallis Newman, 2002   2002.199.11a, b

PAGES 172–73:
Pumps
Susan Bennis/Warren Edwards, American, 1977–9?
Leather, 1985
Brooklyn Museum Costume Collection at The Metropolitan Museum
of Art, Gift of the Brooklyn Museum, 2009; Gift of Candice Gold, 1993
2009.300.1631a, b

PAGE 174:
Pumps
Tokio Kumagaï, Japanese, 1948–1987
Leather, ca. 1986
Brooklyn Museum Costume Collection at The Metropolitan Museum
of Art, Gift of the Brooklyn Museum, 2009; Gift of Candice Gold, 1993
2009.300.3904a, b

PAGE 175:
Pumps
Tokio Kumagaï, Japanese, 1948–1987
Leather, late 1980s
Gift of Jamee Gregory, 2005   2005.322.12a, b

PAGE 176:
The Great Family
René Magritte, French, 1898–1967
Oil on canvas, 39⅜ x 31⅞ in., 1963
PRIVATE COLLECTION
Art © 2011 C. Herscovici, London/Artists Rights Society (ARS), New York
Photograph: Photothèque R. Magritte—ADAGP/Art Resource, New York

PAGE 177:
Pumps
Armando Pollini, Italian
Leather, 1986
Gift of International Museum of Fashion, 1986   1986.258.3a, b

PAGES 178–79:
"Goya" Shoes
Roger Vivier, French, 1913–1998
Leather, silk, metal, fall/winter 1986–87
Gift of Mary Robertson, 2006   2007.211.1a, b

PAGE 180:
Pumps
Isabel Canovas, French, b. 1945
Silk, metal, 1988
Gift of Richard Martin, 1993   1993.34a, b

PAGE 181:
Shoes
Isabel Canovas, French, b. 1945
Silk, leather, spring/summer 1989
Gift of Isabel Canovas, 1989   1989.208.1a, b

PAGES 182–83:
Boots
Andrea Pfister, French (b. Italy), b. 1942
Leather, ca. 1990
Gift of Muriel Kallis Newman, 2005   2005.130.25a, b

PAGE 184:
*Naomi Campbell falls while modeling designs by
Vivienne Westwood,* 1993
Photograph: Rex USA

PAGE 185:
"Portrait" Shoes
Vivienne Westwood, British, b. 1941
Leather, 1990
Millia Davenport and Zipporah Fleisher Fund, 2006   2006.14a, b

PAGES 186–87:
Evening Shoes
Manolo Blahnik, British (b. Spain), b. 1942
Silk, leather, rhinestones, 1990–92
Brooklyn Museum Costume Collection at The Metropolitan Museum of
Art, Gift of the Brooklyn Museum, 2009; Gift of Manolo Blahnik, 1992
2009.300.1630a, b

PAGE 188:
Mules
Manolo Blahnik, British (b. Spain), b. 1942
Silk, leather, fall/winter 2005–06
Gift of Manolo Blahnik, 2006   2006.512.1a, b

PAGE 189:
Manolo Blahnik, 2009
Photograph: Jb Reed/Bloomberg via Getty Images

PAGES 190–91:
"Thorn" Evening Sandals
Roger Vivier, French, 1913–1998; Delman, American, founded 1919,
manufacturer
Silk, metal, spring/summer 1993
Brooklyn Museum Costume Collection at The Metropolitan Museum
of Art, Gift of the Brooklyn Museum, 2009; Gift of Stanley and Murray
Silverstein, Nina Footwear, 1993   2009.300.1633a, b

PAGE 192:
Karl Lagerfeld, 2010
Photograph: Pascal Le Segretain/Getty Images

PAGE 193:
Boots
Karl Lagerfeld, French (b. Germany), b. 1938, for House of Chanel,
French, founded 1913
Synthetic, rubber, metal, fall/winter 1993–94
Purchase, The Dorothy Strelsin Foundation Inc. Gift, 2007   2007.17a, b

PAGES 194–95:
Mules
Bernard Figueroa, American
Leather, synthetic, ca. 1994
Brooklyn Museum Costume Collection at The Metropolitan Museum of
Art, Gift of the Brooklyn Museum, 2009; Gift of Bernard Figueroa, 1996
2009.300.3911a, b

PAGES 196–97:
"Munster" Platform Shoes
John Fluevog, Canadian, b. 1948
Leather, metal, 1994
Gift of Richard Martin, 1994   1994.578.1a, b

PAGE 198:
Ankle Boots
Byron Lars, American, b. 1965
Leather, wood, spring/summer 1994
Gift of Byron Lars, 1997   1997.246c, d

PAGE 199:
Yukihira and Two Brinemaidens at Suma (detail)
Okumura Masanobu, Japanese, 1686–1764
Hanging scroll; ink and color on silk, 33⅛ x 12⅞ in., 18th century
The Harry G. C. Packard Collection of Asian Art, Gift of Harry G. C. Packard,
and Purchase, Fletcher, Rogers, Harris Brisbane Dick, and Louis V. Bell
Funds, Joseph Pulitzer Bequest, and The Annenberg Fund Inc. Gift, 1975
1975.268.126

PAGES 200–01:
"On Liberty" Ensemble
Vivienne Westwood, British, b. 1941
Wool, cotton, leather, fall/winter 1994–95
Gift of Vivienne Westwood, 1995   1995.213a–h

PAGES 202–03:
Sandals
Christian Louboutin, French, b. 1963
Leather, synthetic, ca. 1995
Gift of Amy Fine Collins, 1998   1998.403.3a, b

PAGE 204:
Shoes
Pleaser, American, founded 1993, manufacturer
Synthetic, 2001
Gift of Harold Koda, 2001   2001.619.2a, b

PAGE 205:
Runway model at Scherer Gonzales Fashion Show, 2008
Photograph: Anita Bugge/WireImage

PAGES 206–07:
"Des Robes qui se Dérobent" Evening Ensemble
Jean Paul Gaultier, French, b. 1952
Silk, glass, synthetic, leather, spring/summer 2001
Purchase, Catharine Breyer Van Bomel Foundation Gift, and funds from
various donors, 2001   2001.455.2a–e

PAGE 208:
"Dot" Boots
Manolo Blahnik, British (b. Spain), b. 1942, and Damien Hirst, British,
b. 1965
Cotton, leather, 2002
Catharine Breyer Van Bomel Foundation Fund, 2003   2003.52a, b

PAGE 209:
An art lover looking at Adrenochrome Semicarbazone Sulfonate *(detail)*,
by Damien Hirst
Art © 2011 Hirst Holdings Limited and Damien Hirst. All rights reserved,
ARS, New York/DACS, London
Photograph: Gerry Penny/AFP/Getty Images

PAGE 210:
Boots
Alexander McQueen, British, 1969–2010
Leather, synthetic, spring/summer 2003
Purchase, Allison Sarofim Gift, 2008   2008.307a–d

PAGE 211:
Alexander McQueen, 2003
Photograph: Matthew Fearn/AFP/Getty Images

PAGE 212:
Sandals
Dolce & Gabbana, Italian, founded 1982
Leather, metal, spring/summer 2003
Gift of Dolce & Gabbana, 2003   2003.355.2a, b

PAGE 213:
Gisele Bündchen modeling designs by Dolce & Gabbana, 2002
Photograph: Gruber/WireImage

PAGE 214:
Evening Dress
Yves Saint Laurent, French (b. Algeria), 1936–2008
Silk, feathers, 1969–70
Gift of Baron Philippe de Rothschild, 1983   1983.619.1a, b

PAGE 215:
Shoe
Yves Saint Laurent, French (b. Algeria), 1936–2008
Feathers, leather, synthetic, 2004
Gift of Yves Saint Laurent, 2005   2005.325.2

PAGES 216–17:
"Bhutan" Shoe
Manolo Blahnik, British (b. Spain), b. 1942
Leather, metal, spring/summer 2006
Gift of Manolo Blahnik, 2006   2006.512.6

PAGE 218:
Platform Shoes
Christian Louboutin, French, b. 1963, for Rodarte, American,
founded 2005
Leather, metal, fall/winter 2008–09
Purchase, Gilles Bensimon Inc. Gift, 2009   2009.422d, e

PAGE 219:
Christian Louboutin, 2010
Photograph: Sean Gallup/Getty Images

PAGE 221:
A worker at the Massaro shoemaker workshop, Paris, 2007
Photograph © Jacky Naegelen/X00198/Reuters/Corbis

PAGE 224:
Evening Shoes
Manolo Blahnik, British (b. Spain), b. 1942
Silk, leather, rhinestones, 1990–92
Brooklyn Museum Costume Collection at The Metropolitan Museum of
Art, Gift of the Brooklyn Museum, 2009; Gift of Manolo Blahnik, 1992
2009.300.1630a, b